Shades of Gray

Discerning the Standard of Christian Ethics

Dr. Ronald L. Bernier

Treasure House

An Imprint of

Destiny Image
P.O. Box 310
Shippensburg, PA 17257

"For where your treasure is
there will your heart be also." Matthew 6:21

ISBN 1-56043-794-4

For Worldwide Distribution
Printed in the U.S.A.

Treasure House books are available through these fine distributors outside the United States:

Christian Growth, Inc.
Jalan Kilang-Timor, Singapore 0315

Successful Christian Living
Capetown, Rep. of South Africa

Lifestream
Nottingham, England

Vision Resources
Ponsonby, Auckland, New Zealand

Rhema Ministries Trading
Randburg, South Africa

WA Buchanan Company
Geebung, Queensland, Australia

Salvation Book Centre
Petaling, Jaya, Malaysia

Word Alive
Niverville, Manitoba, Canada

Acknowledgments

Heartfelt thanks are due to many who have labored with me in completing this book...

...to my wife Bernice who is my best friend and sounding board;

to my two children Peter and Andrea who allowed me time for prayer, study, and writing;

to some dear friends and coworkers, Joy Cawley, Charlene Robillard, Dr. Harvey and Joanne Lescault, who helped in the editing process;

to my mom for always expressing interest and encouragement;

to my pastor, Rev. Antone Saraiva, and his wife Carol, for having a vision to build a local church with a biblical pattern for Christian education;

to special friends Gordon, Bev, Bill, and Maria for your many prayers;

to my Lord Jesus Christ who enabled me through His Holy Spirit to accomplish His will and by whose grace I stand.

Contents

Author's Note: The following Bible abbreviations are used on page 19: NEB for the New English Bible; RSV for the Revised Standard Version; JB for Jerusalem Bible; KJV for the King James Version; TEV for Today's English Version; and NIV for the New International Version.

Foreword

The book you are now holding is long overdue. Never has there been such a lack of biblical understanding concerning ethics. There are ninety-nine shades of gray, with everyone vying for legitimacy. But when it comes to what really works we have to go back to the Word of God. The Scriptures tell us to "see to it that no one takes you captive through hollow and deceptive philosophy, which depends on human tradition and the basic principles of this world rather than on Christ" (Col. 2:8, NIV).

Today we live in a humanistic society where the philosophies of man pervade our culture and the Church. Without a clear understanding of a Christian worldview on life, which includes government, education, justice, business, science, etc., we are vulnerable to every wind of philosophy that comes our way.

This book gives a very clear distinction between a Christian view and the world's view that all should understand and have defined in their minds. It is a must for every leader's library.

Dick Iverson
Senior Pastor,
Bible Temple, Portland, Oregon

Preface

Why is it that today so many are swayed by mere emotionalism or trapped by the most recent propaganda disseminated through television or in the classroom? While there are several factors, one that stands out is that people do not think critically. In 2 Corinthians 10:5 (NIV), the apostle Paul writes, "We demolish arguments and every pretension that sets itself up against the knowledge of God, and we take captive every thought to make it obedient to Christ." If we are to take every thought captive we must learn to think! As Christians, we are to follow the example of the Christians at Berea. They were of "more noble character" because "they received the message with great eagerness and examined the Scriptures every day to see if what Paul said was true" (Acts 17:11, NIV). Paul also exhorted the Colossian church to "See to it that no one takes you captive through hollow and deceptive philosophy, which depends on human tradition and the basic principles of this world rather than on Christ" (Col. 2:8, NIV). As Christians we need to be able to discern what standard of evaluation we will use to make our day to day decisions.

The foundation for logical thinking is the law of noncontradiction. The law may be stated as follows: a statement cannot be true and not true at the same time and in the same respect. Throughout the Bible, the law of noncontradiction is implied. If it were not, then nothing would be a claim to truth. Right thinking is thinking that imitates God's thinking. God's revealed law, which is part of the law of nature, is to be found only in the Holy Scriptures.

Sometimes we have heard it said that you can't legislate morality. Some have even made the statement that religion should be kept separate from law. Those statements are ridiculous. Every law is a legislation of morality, because law sets a standard of what is acceptable. The only issue is what will be the standard? What will be the religion that determines what the law is? We either live in obedience to God and follow His Word for our entire legal system, or we put up a man-made substitute. If we change the theological base of a legal system, we will change its government, its families, its education, etc. (see Deut. 4:5-9). However, if we don't obey God's Word, we will pay the consequences.

The most insidious humanistic philosophy being perpetrated on us today is called relativism. Relativism is the belief that there is absolutely no absolute. Relativism says, "to each his own." In the eyes of a relativist, the greatest evil that you can commit is being close-minded, intolerant, or judgmental. Every law in our country is based on a concept of morality. For the Christian and non-Christian the morality dictated by the Ten Commandments holds society together and governs us and is the basis of any just legal system. The question isn't whether morality or values are going to be part of our society. The question is whose values are going to rule our society? When you take a "neutral" position between good and evil, you are in a position which directly supports and encourages evil.

In the subsequent chapters we will be studying what is ethics, what are some of the prevailing philosophies that affect our thinking, why it is important to understand worldview, Antinomianism and its humanistic contribution to the relativism of today, and finally a foundation for a biblical way of life. To make a difference, we must know what we believe and why we believe it. James Sire wrote in his book *The Universe Next Door*[1] that "to be a Christian theist is not just to have an intellectual world view; it is to be personally committed to the infinite-personal Lord of the Universe. And it leads to an examined life that is well worth living." My prayer is that this book will help you live out Paul's exhortation to the Romans, "Do not conform any longer to the pattern of this world, but be transformed by the renewing of your mind. Then you will be able to test and approve what God's will is— His good, pleasing and perfect will" (Rom. 12:2, NIV).

Dr. Ronald L. Bernier

---

1. James W. Sire, *The Universe Next Door* (Downers Grove, Illinois: InterVarsity Press, 1988).

Introduction—
Ethics Defined

According to G.W. Bromiley, ethics is to be considered a universal entity since "all cultures and religions have customs, practices, traditions, and modes of conduct."[2] "The word ethic is derived from the Greek word *ethos*, which means habit of custom."[3] "In Greece, of course, 'ethics' originally had the general sense of customs. Latin *mos* (pl. *mores*, from which Eng. "morality" derives) bears a similar sense."[4]

Webster's Dictionary defines ethic as the "principle of right or good behavior; a system of moral principles

---

2. G.W. Bromiley, "Philosophical Ethics: Nature and Function," *The International Standard Bible Encyclopedia* (Grand Rapids, Michigan: Eerdmans, reprinted 1988) Vol. 2, p.183.
3. Taken from the book, CHOICES OF THE HEART by Douglas D. Webster. Used by permission of Zondervan Publishing House.
4. Bromiley, op. cit.

or values" and ethics as "the study of the general nature of morals and the specific moral choices an individual makes in relating to others."[5]

The development of modern ethics is more in keeping with the derivation of the world than the ancient tradition of Christian theology that founded ethics on God's unchanging, eternally relevant moral wisdom. Today's ethos, with its accent on **utilitarian and expressive individualism,** conditions behavior to a new standard of success, freedom, and self-fulfillment.[6]

"Now ethics and morals are related as theory and practice; thus 'ethics' is the study (or systematization) of morals, while 'morals' (or "morality") means the actual conduct of people viewed with concern for right and wrong, good and evil, virtue and vice."[7]

Webster's Dictionary defines ethic as a principle of right or good behavior, a system of moral principles or values, and ethics as the study of the general nature of morals and the specific moral choices an individual makes in relating to others.

When thoughtful people began to question traditional modes of behavior in the light of new

5. *Webster's II New Riverside University Dictionary* (Boston, Massachusetts: The Riverside Publishing Company, 1984), p. 445.
6. Webster, op. cit. p. 37.
7. James Wm. McClendon, Jr., *Ethics: Systematic Theology* (Nashville, Tennessee: Abingdon Press, 1986), Vol. 1, p. 47.

situations, interest, and concerns, this questioning took three related forms, which have become normative in ethical discussion. First, **what is the basis of action?** On what ground ought one to do this action and not do another? Second, **what is the criterion of evaluation?** Is there some absolute or only a relative rule or principle by which to judge? Third, **what is the goal of human conduct?** What end or ends would actions serve?[8]

What is the basis of action?

On what ground ought one to do this action and not do another?

What is the criterion of evaluation?

Is there some absolute or only a relative rule or principle to judge?

What is the goal of human conduct?

What end or ends should actions serve?

Many theories have been proposed, developed, and practiced to try to answer the above questions concerning what is morally good action. Man's quest to acquire knowledge of good and evil is rooted in the Adamic deception which took place at the foot of the tree of good and evil (see Gen. 2:15-17; 3:1-24). The quest in and of itself may be viewed as morally good. However, God is the source of truth, knowledge, and goodness; therefore, truth, knowledge, and goodness

---

8.   Bromiley, op. cit.

can only be revealed through Him. What seems to be lacking in the ethical views which are in contrast to the Christian view of morality is the presence of an unchanging standard—the presence of the unchanging standard being the central point of the Christian view of morality.

In our discussion here, we will survey many of the theories concerning morality which attempt to delineate the basis for man's actions, the criterion by which man evaluates what is good and what is evil, and the goal of human conduct. Since all cultures and societies function within one or more ethical systems, it would seem an important task for each of us to define the ethic by which we make our day-to-day decisions about what is good and what is evil—only one bears an unchanging standard.

Since all cultures and societies function within one or more ethics, it would seem an important task for each of us to define the ethic by which we make our day-to-day decisions about what is good and what is evil—only one bears an unchanging standard.

Discussion Questions

1. In the preface the author writes that as Christians we need to be able to discern what will be the standard of evaluation we will use to make our day-to-day decisions.

   How does a differing standard affect our decision-making process?
2. How does critical thinking enable us in decision making?
3. Consider the three related forms of questioning used in the normative ethical discussion listed in the introduction.

   What answers might you provide to these questions?
   a. What is the basis for your actions?

   b. What is the criterion of your evaluation?

   c. What is the goal of your human conduct?

Chapter 1

Prevailing Philosophies

Justice Is in the Interest of the Stronger Party

Thrasymachus, an ancient Greek philosopher, taught that the permanent element in morality is "the interest of the strongest party. In other words, what is morally right is defined in terms of who has the power."[1]

What is morally right is defined in terms of who has the power.

This theory poses many problems. What does power have to do with what is right? Can both a right action and a wrong action be done by one who has the

---

1.   Norman L. Geisler, *Christian Ethics: Options and Issues.* (Grand Rapids, Michigan: Baker Book House, 1990), p. 17.

greater power? Is one who is not powerful able to do good? This "might is right" theory does not reconcile the difference between strength and goodness. The Bible teaches us that we can be declared good (righteous) in our weakness because Christ is our strength if we believe (see Rom. 5:5-8,18-19). Our strength is not to be used for our own gain, but for the lifting up of those not so strong (see Rom. 15:1).

Right Is What the Community Says Is Right

This theory of ethics states that the determination of what is morally right is dependent upon the needs of the community to which one belongs. Each community would define what is right according to its own needs. "Community demands are the ethical commands."[2] The fallacy of this principle of determining "right" is that what may be truly right has little to do with the way a certain community may act or think.

Each community defines what is right according to its own needs.

Sodom and Gomorrah are an example of this in that the whole community was involved in wrong behavior and was destroyed in judgment, a sign of future judgments for others who would practice such acts. The other problem that would develop if each community determined what was right is that there would be no means of settling disputes between communities

---

2.   Ibid. p. 18.

when conflicting thoughts occurred. We do not live in isolated bubbles so that members of one society never come into contact with members of another society. Never in any time of history has there been such an ability to travel and interact with people in every area of the globe. Communications through television, radio, telephone, computers, and satellites have become a normal way of life. Information from anywhere in the world can reach your home in a matter of minutes. With this in mind, can you imagine travelling to different places only to find that the actions you have come to accept as morally good are considered unacceptable? This would lead to a state of confusion for all of us, and there would be no way of resolving any conflict. Contradicting thoughts cannot all be true. Everyone cannot be right. There must be some other measure of what is right.

Man Is the Measure

"Protagoras[1], an ancient Greek philosopher, claimed that "man is the measure of all things." Understood as pertaining to individuals, this means that each person's own will is the standard for what is right and wrong.[3] This gives each man the power to determine what is right for him. Right then can only be defined in relation to someone's will. If two people have conflicting wills (and they do), then they will have conflicting views on what is right.

---

3.   Ibid.

Each person's will is the standard for what is right and wrong.

The Book of Judges speaks of a time when Israel had no kings and everyone did what was right in his own eyes. When this is put into practice, society ceases to operate, resulting in chaos. Unity becomes an unattainable goal; man becomes a god unto himself and worships the god of his making. Because man's will is subject to change, depending on circumstances in his life, then what he believes to be morally right is also subject to change. Thus, we find that in the end man doesn't have unity even in himself. In man there is no consistent place to begin the "measure" of things.

Mankind Is the Measure of All Things

In this type of ethical thinking, the race as a whole is used to determine what is right. Mankind replaces God because He is unknowable. Government (the expression and representation of the dominate social class) becomes the institution of salvation and legislates what is right.

The race as a whole is used to determine what is right.

Can the whole or a majority of people determine what is right? If society changes, does what is right also change with that society? Can man do and know what is right without a standard that is outside himself? If man and society are continually changing, can any standard be true for any given society if it is only determined by that society? History gives us many examples to indicate that even the whole of a community could be wrong.

There must be a perfect standard by which what is right can be determined, so that what is right is consistent through all generations.

There must be a perfect standard by which what is right can be determined, so that what is right is consistent through all generations.

Morality Is Found in Moderation

This philosophy, attributed to Aristotle[2], permeates many areas of our thinking. The right balance of food, exercise, work, play, family, church, friends, and sleep would constitute a moderate course of action. In fact, moderation is a wise course of action. We all need a proper balance with which to live life. But is this proper balance a description of morality? Is taking time for all of life's disciplines necessarily living a good and moral life? Can one be moderate and still wrong? Can one be moderate and still immoral?

Aristotle strongly urges *moderation* in all things, for the immoderate act is immoral or vicious. Extremes are always evil, whether it be the extreme of deficiency or that of excess. Between these two extremes, a virtue will be found. When one cannot hold to the dead center of a mean, then he is advised to lean to the side of the lesser evil, to choose the lesser of the two evils. ...Every true virtue, as a mean between extremes, impels man to live in harmony with reason, to live a rational life. The moderate, right act means doing the right thing to the right person, at the right time, to the right extent, with the right purpose, in the right manner. Thus, right doing is not within the reach of everyone, but only of the one equipped with the knowledge and ability to make the correct choice and discovering the truth—just as not everyone can be expected to find the exact center of a circle.[4]

Norman Geisler describes three reasons why this thinking is not the very nature of what is good.

First of all, many times the right thing is the extreme thing to do. In emergencies, in self-defense, and in wars against aggression, moderate actions are not always the best ones. Even some virtues obviously should not be expressed in moderate amounts. One should not be moderately loving. Neither should we be moderately grateful, thankful, or generous. *Second, there is not universal agreement on what is moderate.* Aristotle, for example, considered humility a vice, Christians believe it to be a virtue. *Third, moderation is at best only a general guide for action, not a universal ethical law.*[5]

Though we might use moderation as an expression of morality, we cannot use moderation as a definition of morality.

4.   William S. Sahakian, *History of Philosophy* (New York, New York: Harper Collins Publishers, 1968), p. 74.
5.   Geisler, op. cit. p. 19.

What Brings Pleasure Is Right

This doctrine, known as hedonism, states that...

...pleasure is the highest good (or the sole good) in life, pleasure is an intrinsic good (or the only intrinsic good), pleasure should be sought, and the ethical worth (value, good) of human actions is determined by whether or not they produce pleasure. Ethical hedonism insists that each individual is obligated to himself to live so as to obtain as much pleasure and as little pain as possible.[6]

Based on this doctrine we can state that what is pleasurable is morally good, and what brings pain is morally wrong.

Based on this doctrine we can state that what is pleasurable is morally good, and what brings pain is morally wrong.

There are many difficulties with this doctrinal position. First, who will determine what is pleasurable—an individual, a group, or an entire race? Can two people having the same experience view that experience differently? When more than one share an experience, who determines if it is pleasurable? You can see the problem of determining what is right based on individual experience of pleasure. Second, in what time frame will pleasure be experienced after a particular action? Is immediate pleasure the criterion or ultimate pleasure? Is

6. Peter A. Angeles, *Dictionary of Philosophy* (New York, New York: Harper Perennial, 1991), p. 114.

it possible that we might incur pain in order to obtain pleasure? Third, what kind of pleasure should be used to determine morality? We can experience physical, psychological, emotional, spiritual, temporal, or eternal pleasure. Some pain that we experience (such as sore muscles from exercise) can even in the end be pleasurable (winning a competition). This hedonistic formula for determining what is good can become very complicated and in the end prove to be more harmful than valuable. As likes and dislikes change, so would what is good.

The Greatest Good for the Greatest Number Is Right

Utilitarianism, sometimes referred to as the great est happiness theory, was introduced as a systematic ethical theory. Following are some of the main tenets of utilitarianism:

1. One should act as to promote the greatest happiness (pleasure) of the greatest number of people. 2. Pleasure is the only intrinsic good and pain is the only intrinsic evil. 3. An act is morally right (a) if it brings about a greater balance of good over evil than any other action that could have been taken, or (b) if it produces as much good in the world as or no less good in the world than would any other act possible under the circumstances.

In general, the moral worth of an act is judged according to the goodness and badness of its consequences.

4. In general, the moral worth of an act is judged according to the goodness and badness of its consequences.[7]

We have already outlined some of the problems associated with a hedonistic approach to what is right; similarly, the problems associated with this utilitarian definition are multiple.

First, there is no agreement on how good should be understood. Some understand the meaning of good quantitatively (Jeremy Bentham [1748-1832]). Others understand it qualitatively (John Stuart Mill [1806-1873]). Second, it begs the question to say that moral right is what brings the greatest "good." Either right and good are defined in terms of each other, which is circular reasoning, or good must be determined by some standard beyond the utilitarian process. Third, no human being can accurately predict what will happen in the long run. Hence, for all practical purposes a utilitarian definition of good is useless. It must still fall back on something else to determine what is good now, in the short run.[8]

The principle of the greatest happiness for the greatest number furnishes a rough-and-ready method of balancing the demands of interest groups.

Theoretically, utilitarianism leaves unanswered the question of what to do with the dissident, the outcast, and the minority.

7. Ibid. p. 307.
8. Geisler, op. cit. p. 20.

Theoretically, utilitarianism leaves unanswered the question of what to do with the dissident, the outcast, and the minority. Utilitarianism is the ethical palliative of an affluent society. Only as other values and ideals are superimposed upon it can utilitarian principles be made to function in a civilized manner.[9]

What Is Right Cannot Be Defined

Although many have tried to propose a viable ethic, we can conclude that man is not able to determine what is right and good in and of himself. "Even when man's life was untainted by sin, his moral consciousness was not ultimate, but derivative; Adam was not without external moral dictate; he knew what was good and evil because his Lord told him. Adam did not look to himself for moral steering; rather, he lived by supernatural, positive revelation."[10]

When we begin believing that we should know good and evil of ourselves, we begin being moral arbitrators determining good and evil. We fall into the same trap that was laid for Adam—deciding to be self-sufficient in our moral consciousness and reasoning, substituting self-rule for God's rule.

---

9. R.K. Harrison, ed., *Encyclopedia of Biblical and Christian Ethics* (Nashville, Tennessee: Thomas Nelson Publishers, 1987), p. 422.
10. Greg L. Bahnsen, *Theonomy in Christian Ethics* (Phillipsburg, New Jersey: Presbyterian and Reformed Publishing Company, 1984), p. 280.

When we begin believing that we should know good and evil of ourselves, we begin being moral arbitrators determining good and evil. We fall into the same trap that was laid for Adam—deciding to be self-sufficient in our moral consciousness and reasoning, substituting self-rule for God's rule. As man we are not morally self-sufficient and when we try to be, we sin and rebel against God.

Good Is What God Wills

What is good can only be determined by the One who is good. "The good is what God wills is good. Whatever action God specifies to be a good action is a good action. ...Thus, moral good is both ultimate and specifiable. It is ultimate because it comes from God. And it is specifiable since it is found in His revelation to mankind."[11]

In any theological development of ethics certain principles must be taken into account.

1. **God, Himself, is the ground of right human action.**

2. **God, Himself, is the norm of right human action.**

3. **God, Himself, is the power of right human action.**

4. **God, Himself, is the goal and purpose of right human conduct.**

---

11.   Geisler, op. cit. p. 21.

In any theological development of ethics certain principles must be taken into account. ...First, God Himself is the ground of right human action. ...Second, God Himself, as ground, is also the norm of right human action. ...Third, God Himself, as ground and norm, is the power of right human action. ...Fourth, God Himself, as ground, norm, and power, is the goal and purpose of right human conduct. ...In relation to goal as well as to ground, norm, and power, Holy Scripture plays a key role, for it is only through the inspired record that God as the goal of human action may be known and accepted, with all that this implies for the direction of life, the course and validity of right action, and the destiny of those who commit themselves to God as their all in all.[12]

Two objections are often raised, first, it is alleged that this view is a form of authoritarianism. This objection, however, is valid only if the authority is less than ultimate. That is, if any finite creature professed to have this ultimate authority, then we could rightly cry "authoritarianism." However, there is nothing wrong with considering the ultimate authority to be the ultimate authority. If an absolutely morally perfect God exists, then by His very nature He is the ultimate authority (or standard) for what is good and what is not. The second objection is that defining good in terms of God's will is arbitrary.

---

12.   Bromiley, op. cit. pp. 189-190.

This objection applies, however, only to a voluntaristic view of good, not to an essentialistic view of good. A voluntarist believes that something is good simply because God wills it. An essentialist, on the other hand, holds that God wills something because it is good in accordance with His own nature.

Only through God's rule can there be an effective moral system, for there is only one Law-giver: the living and true God.

This latter form of the divine-command view of ethics escapes these criticisms and forms the basis of a Christian ethic.[13]

Only through God's rule can there be an effective moral system, for there is only one Law-giver: the living and true God. All forms of self-rule refuse to acknowledge this.

> The autonomous philosopher is misled in his metaphysical and, hence, epistemological presuppositions. Presuming autonomy he does not see the facts of God's self-sufficient authority over man and His self-attesting communication to man; it is only inevitable, then, that he will be misled in his ethics. In fact, the very presumption of self-sufficiency is evidence of immorality, sinful rebellion against the clearly revealed, living and true God. When man turns away from covenantal theonomy to supposed autonomy, ethics become a vain delusion.[14]

---

13.   Geisler, op. cit. pp. 21-22.

Discussion Questions

1. Consider one or more of the prevailing philosophies listed in Chapter 1 and discuss how a society built totally on one of these philosophies would function in our modern world and how would it affect you in the way you live today? (Consider your home life, school, work, recreation, church, etc.)

2. What is the result of differing people who subscribe to differing philosophies all trying to function in a social structure? What happens when there is disagreement?

3. If you were to set up a governmental system for the protection and well being of society, what would be the foundation for your legislation?

---

14.   Bahnsen, op. cit. p. 281.

Chapter 2

Conflicting Worldviews

Students of history realized that no society can survive, no civilization can function, without some unifying system of thought. All societies are made up of different people, different jobs, different values, and different classes. In a broad sense, all societies are melting pots.

How do the parts fit together to make a whole? What makes a society a unified system? Some kind of glue is required in order for the parts to stick together. The glue is found in a unifying system of thought, what we call a "worldview."[1]

---

1. R.C. Sproul, *Lifeviews* (Old Tappan, New Jersey: Fleming H. Revell Company, 1986), p. 29.

Jesus Christ knew the critical importance of worldview. His statements to His followers about listening and seeing were centered around *how* more than *what* they looked at and listened to: Therefore consider carefully **how** you listen. Whoever has will be given more; whoever does not have, even what he thinks he has will be taken from him (Lk. 8:18). The eye is the lamp of the body. If your eyes are good, your whole body will be full of light. But if your eyes are bad, your whole body will be full of darkness. If then the light within you is darkness, how great is that darkness! (Mt. 6:22-23)[2]

Herbert Schlossberg and Marvin Olasky wrote in *Turning Point: A Christian Worldview Declaration* that...

...a biblical worldview gives us a clear look at reality. When we move away from that clear view, we are like children increasingly smudging a window with dirty fingerprints and then looking outside. First the colors become duller. Then the shape begins to alter. As the dirt gets thicker, the light is progressively shut out. It becomes harder to say with accuracy what is happening out there. If the process takes place gradually, we might hardly notice what is happening, but increasingly we are cut off from reality.... To the extent that our worldview departs from God's message to us, our perceptions are distorted.[3]

---

2. Taken from *Generation at Risk* by Fran Sciacca. Copyright 1990, Fran Sciacca. Moody Press. Used by permission.

As we begin to walk away from God's truth, we walk away from the sacred toward the secular. The dominant philosophy or worldview in opposition to the biblical worldview in our contemporary age is Secularism.

"Secularism is the umbrella that shields the various competing philosophies beneath it. Secularism has the necessary common denominator to tie together humanism, pluralism, existentialism, and several other 'isms.' "[4]

> Secular comes from the Latin *saeculum*, meaning "time" or "age," and thus secularism is a view of life that causes the secularist to be totally of this age, without any vision for eternity. It maintains that, as history moves on, so values and rules, laws and norms, change. Thus morality is merely that accepted or tolerated by the society in which one lives. For secularism, morality cannot consist of norms, values, and laws dictated by religious faith; it must be worked out freely and chosen by people for themselves. While secularism is a philosophy of life, secularization is a social process that both prepares the way for, and actually aids, the former. Secularism may be viewed either as a body of teaching or as a set of assumptions that insist that the real meaning of this world is found within itself, that we need not concern ourself with any further life, and that

3. Herbert Schlossberg and Marvin Olasky, as quoted in Sciacca, ibid.
4. Sproul, op. cit. p. 32.

morality can be based on these worldly principles rather than on claims of revealed truth.[5]

The philosopher, who refuses to acknowledge God's rule, claiming autonomy, is misled in his ethics. Not seeing God's rule over man or His self-attesting communication to man, the autonomous philospher considers only the natural and secular.

Harry Blamires has written a book entitled *The Christian Mind.* In his first chapter entitled "The Surrender to Secularism" he says such things as "...the mind of modern man has been secularized...it has been deprived of any orientation towards the supernatural." He goes on to express the following very meaningful and disturbing truths about what has happened, even to Christians, in this education tension: "But as a thinking being, the modern Christian has succumbed to secularization. He accepts religion—its morality, its worship, its spiritual culture; but he rejects the religious view of life, the view, which sets all earthly issues within the context of the eternal, the view which relates all human problems—social, political, cultural—to the doctrinal foundations of the Christian faith, the view which sees all things here below in terms of God's supremacy and earth's transitoriness, in terms of Heaven and Hell. ...One knows Christian acquaintances with whom one cannot broach any educational topic because they cannot conceive that any policy or practice

---

5.   R.K. Harrison, ed., *Encyclopedia of Biblical and Christian Ethics* (Nashville, Tennessee: Thomas Nelson Publishers, 1987), p. 368.

could be open to question which has the backing of secular Establishment."[6]

As society increasingly violates divine principles, such transgression soon becomes a matter of common practice and public acceptance....

Moral rebellion, the Bible warns us, runs a quickly accelerating course. When repeated compromise erodes God's norms of decency, respect for God soon yields to false gods that encourage sin and accommodate evil. God will permit a rebellious generation to suffer "the vileness of their own desires, and the constant degradation of their bodies, because they have bartered away the true God for a false one..." (Rom. 1:24-25, NEB).

Refusal to honor God leads inevitably to destructive after shock: "Thinking has ended in futility, and...misguided minds are plunged in darkness" (Rom. 1:21, NEB). God gives them over, Scripture says, to "a base mind and to improper conduct" (Rom. 1:28, RSV); to "their own irrational ideas and to their monstrous behavior" (JB); to a "reprobate" mind (KJV); to a "degenerate" mind (Phillips); to a "corrupted" mind (TEV); to a "depraved" mind (NIV).[7]

---

6.   From *The Christian Mind,* © 1963 by Harry Blaires. Published by Servant Publications, Box 8617, Ann Arbor, Michigan 48107. Used with permission. As quoted in Walter O. Ediger, *The Quest for Excellence in Christian School Education* (Siloah Springs, Arizona: RPA Associates, 1993) pp. 21-22.

7.   Carl F.H. Henry, *The Christian Mindset in a Secular Society* (Portland, Oregon: Multnomah Press, 1984), pp. 144-145.

The Morality of God

Genesis 1:26-27 "Let us make man in our image according to our likeness...male and female He created them."

Roman 16:19 "I want you to be wise in what is good and innocent in what is evil."

God Created Man to be:

Conformed to be the image of Jesus Christ (Romans 8:29)

To know:

The truth and the truth shall make you free (John 8:32).

1. Truth is an eternal unchanging statement or principle that is in agreement with reality.

2. God's Word is Truth (2 Thess. 2:10).

3. Truth is revealed to us by God Himself.

General Revelation (Psalm 19:1)

Special Revelation (2 Peter 1:21)

Incarnate Revelation (John 1:14)

4. Truth is objectively comprehensible by man (Heb. 5:14).

5. Truth is authoritative yet cohesive and should produce unity.

6. God is Truth (1 Cor. 1:18).

7. Jesus Christ is Truth (John 14:6).

8. The Holy Spirit is Truth (John 14:17).

To do

The will of God...which is good and acceptable and perfect (Romans 12:2)

The Morality of Satan

Genesis 3:5 "You shall not die...You will be like God knowing good and evil."

Romans 1:21-25 "They knew God but did not honor Him as God or give thanks; they became fools...they exchanged the truth of God for a lie and worshipped and served the creature rather than the Creator who is blessed forever."

Results of Immorality

1. God sends upon them a deluding influence so that they might believe what is false in order that all may be judged who did not believe the truth but took pleasure in wickedness (2 Thessalonians 2:11-12).

2. God gives them over in the lusts of their hearts to impurity (Romans 1:24).

3. God gives them over to degrading passions (Romans 1:26).

4. God gives them over to a depraved mind to do those things which are not proper (Romans 1:28-31).

Unrightesouness	slanderers
malice	insolent
strife	unloving
gossips	greed
haters of God	murder
inventors of evil	malice
disobedient to parents	arrogant
without understnading	boastful
wickedness	unmerciful
full of envy	untrustworthy
deceit	

5. They give hearty approval to all who practice evil (Romans 1:32).

6. The wages of sin is death (Romans 6:23).

Figure 1

The contrast of the morality of God in which He has purposed man to walk and the morality of satan, who is the liar and deceives man into thinking he can be God, is illustrated in Figure 1. God's purpose for man is to be conformed to the image of Jesus Christ (Rom. 8:29), to know the truth, and that truth will bring freedom (see Jn. 8:32), and to do the will of God, which is good, acceptable, and perfect (see Rom. 12:2). The biblical world-view reveals to man his origin, destination, and purpose, beginning in times past, extending into all eternity. The secular man can only know this time and place; he does not know his purpose, beginning, or destiny; therefore, he organizes himself only in regard to the present. When we exchange the truth of God for the lie of the creature (see Rom. 1:21-25), we begin a moral slide.

> Man's first step in defecting from God who makes known His holy will is to replace the immortal God with mortal man (Rom. 1:23). The ancients worshipped emperors, even their statues; moderns worship the self as the measure of all things. This self-worship is actually a divine judgment upon us for rejecting the one true God. Such deliberate idolatry of the self quickly moves on to the unbridled passion characteristic of our times.[8]

As man is separated from God, he experiences broken fellowship, broken covenant, and broken relationship (see Gen. 3:1-19) causing a great gulf of

---

8.   Ibid. p. 146.

separation (see Lk. 16:19-26), and man's ability to communicate with a Holy God is severed. To the man who is separated from God by sin, the heavens remain closed (see Deut. 28:23; Lev. 26:19; 2 Chron. 6:26; Mal. 3:10). Figure 2 displays the chain of divine communication. God's purpose for man is that he might receive the revelation of God through the redemption of Jesus. It is through the means of redemption that man can be restored to God and find purpose, not only for the now, but for all eternity.

1	2	3
Communication in creation before sin.	**Communication gap by transgression after sin**	**Communication in redemption-gap bridged**
God-Fellowship-Man	**God-Gulf-Man**	**God-Christ-Man**
"Open Heavens"	**"Closed Heavens"**	**"Gap Bridged"**
Ex. 24:9-11	Deut. 28:23	Heb. 10:22; 12:22
Ezek1:1	Lev. 26:19	Ex. 25:22 "I Wills"
Gen. 28:12-14	1 Kgs. 8	1. Meet with you
Jn. 1:51	2 Chron. 6:26	2. Commune with you
Mt. 3:16	Mal. 3:10	3. Give you Figure 2

James Orr(1) outlined a sketch of the Christian view of the world in nine statements which became the basis for a series of lectures. He considered that...

...the Christian view of the world affirms:

1. The existence of a Personal, Ethical, Self-Revealing God. It is thus at the outset a system of Theism, and as such is opposed to all systems of Atheism, Agnosticism, Pantheism, or mere Deism.

2. The creation of the world by God, His immanent presence in it, His transcendence over it, and

His holy and wise government of it for moral ends.

3. The spiritual nature and dignity of man—his creation in the Divine image, and destination to bear the likeness of God in a perfected relation of sonship.

4. The fact of sin and disorder of the world, not as something belonging to the Divine idea of it, and inherent in it by necessity, but as something which has entered it by the voluntary turning aside of man from his allegiance to his Creator, and from the path of his normal development. The Christian view of the world, in other words, involves a Fall as the presupposition of its doctrine of Redemption; whereas the "modern" view of the world affirms that the so-called Fall was in reality a rise, and denies by consequence the need of Redemption in the scriptural sense.

5. The historical Self-Revelation of God to the patriarchs and in the line of Israel, and, as brought to light by this, a gracious purpose of God for the salvation of the world, centering in Jesus Christ, His Son, and the new Head of humanity.

6. That Jesus Christ was not mere man, but the eternal Son of God—a truly Divine Person—who in the fulness of time took upon Himself our humanity, and who, on the ground that in Him as man there dwells the fulness of the

Godhead bodily, is to be honored, worshipped, and trusted, even as God is. This is the transcendent "mystery of godliness"—the central and amazing assertion of the Christian view—by reference to which our relation is determined to everything else which it contains.

7. The Redemption of the world through a great act of Atonement—this Atonement to be appropriated by faith, and availing for all who do not willfully withstand and reject its grace.

8. That the historical aim of Christ's work was the founding of a Kingdom of God on earth, which includes not only the spiritual salvation of individuals, but a new order of society, the result of the action of the spiritual forces set in motion through Christ.

9. That history has a goal, and that the present order of things will be terminated by the appearance of the Son of Man for judgment, the resurrection of the dead, and the final separation of righteous and wicked—final, so far as the Scriptures afford any light, or entitle us to hold out any hope.

Beyond this are the eternal ages, on whose depths only stray lights fall, as in that remarkable passage— "Then cometh the end, when He shall have delivered up the kingdom to God, even the Father...then shall the Son also Himself be subject unto Him that put all things under Him, that God may be all in all" (1 Cor. 15:24,28) and on the mysterious blessedness or sorrow of which, as the case may be, it is needless to speculate.[9]

We can begin to understand a Christian worldview as an ability to receive revelation of a transcendent God who is also immanent (existing or remains within) in His creation (Figure 3). He is not only transcendent, that is, above and beyond the natural order, but He is also immanent in the world, that is, He pervades every aspect of His creation and actively rules over all created existence.

Christian Worldview

GOD
Supernatural
(Invisible)

Transcendence
"Above and beyond the
natural order"

Revelation
Sacred   ⇓
⇑ (Extraordinary)

Immanent
"He pervades every
aspect of his creation
and actively rules over
all created existences."
1. Being
2. History
3. Incarnation
4. Holy Spirit

Reason
Natural
WORLD

Secular
(ordinary)

Figure 3

9.   James Orr, *The Christian View of God and the World* (Grand Rapids, Michigan: Kregel Publications, reprinted 1989), pp. 32-34.

The secular worldview says we cannot know God (there is a great gulf), He has closed off the heavens; so let us organize our thoughts as though He did not even exist (Figure 4). In secularism, not only is the relationship between God and the natural order erased, but there is also a barrier between them. No longer are there any "self-evident truths," only "opinions." No longer is there any unity, only diversity; no longer any absolutes, only relativity. With the breakdown of man's access to God and the relationship of the secular to the sacred, alienation has consequently occurred at every level of human relations as well.

Because of these worldviews being in contrast to each other, they pervade our beliefs in many aspects of our lives (see Chart 1 and Chart 2).

We live out our beliefs. The danger in assessing these individual beliefs without looking at the entire worldview is that we might pick and choose what is right based on preference.

The theologians who have sought to combine Christianity and secularism are on a fool's errand. It cannot be done. The root concepts of Christianity cannot be unified with the root concepts of secularism. If we seek to breed them, the result will be a grotesque hybrid. It will be sterile, like a mule, powerless to reproduce. If we seek to effect a synthesis between two radically conflicting world views, we must inevitably submerge one into the other. The result of such bastardization can be neither Christianity nor secularism. If a Christian buys into secularism his world view is no longer Christian. If a secularist buys into Christianity, he is no longer a secularist.[10]

Secularist Worldview

GOD

Supernatural
(Invisible)

Revelation
↓
Unity-Universals-Absolutes

BARRICADE
Gulf-Wall-"Closed Heavens"
Diversity-Particulars-Relative

⇑

Reason (Can't know God)

Natural
(Visible)

World
Secular
Secularism advocates denial of the super-natural—this time and this place are all there is.

When man is separated from God there remains a great gulf fix (Lk. 16:19-26) due to broken fellow-ship, broken covenant and broken relation-ship (Gen. 3:1-19) resulting in a closed Heaven.

Deut. 28:23
Lev. 26:19
2 Chron. 6:26
Mal. 3:10

Man's divorce from God causes him to build philosophies based on self rule.

The problem is not knowledge it is knowledge without God

Figure 4

---

10.   Sproul, op. cit. p. 38.

Western society tends toward a dualism that
divides life between the sacred and the secular.
The Kingdom of God is identified with the Church
while the rest of life is seen as secular. Christians tend to be culture responders rather than
culture initiators. This results in various view
points on how Christ and culture are to relate.
...The Christian world-view and life style is
aimed at penetrating culture at all levels through
winsome, knowledgeable, patient, loving, and
persistent relationships. Christians hold dual
citizenship, both in the City of God and the City
of Man. Neither must be neglected, even though
the former takes priority. Our Lord impacted
His culture. He ate with publicans and sinners;
He paid taxes; He met people's needs at all
levels and demonstrated by His life and activities the meaning of His words. He was not
deceived by the worldly cultures of either the
pharisaical legalistic culture or the Roman
secular one."[11]

Since then we cannot intermarry a Christian
worldview with a secular worldview and end up with
the Christian ethic, it would be important to distin-
guish any philosophy that distorts or nullifies a
Christian worldview so that the ethic to which we
subscribe is in fact Christian.

One philosophy which has oftentimes brought distortion to the Christian worldview, is Antinomianism.

---

11.   James D. Cunningham and Anthony C. Fortosis, *Education
      in Christian Schools: A Perspective and "Training Model"*
      (Whittier, California: the Association of Christian Schools In-
      ternational, 1987), pp. 130-132.

Classical/Biblical

God

Self-existent and pre-existent; transcendent and immanent; absolute and sovereign creator; revealed in nature and Scripture

Religion

Based on revelation (nature and Scripture).

Church

The divine instituion of redemption; "the Body of Christ" comprising community of faithful

Science

All viewed terms of createdness; world is cosmos, not chaos; "think God's thoughts after Him." (Newton)

Government

Created by God as servant of Divine government; Church and state separate, but not God and State

Law

All human laws derived from eternal norms of God's laws

Nature

Created by God, nature is thus a vehicle of divine revelation

Life

Life sacramental (sacred); loss of man's significance greatest loss of 20th century

The Arts

Bear witness to the Creator—the true, the good, the beautiful

Work

Corum Deo ("before the face of God"); joy in serving God in every kind of work as a divine appointment; an eternal reward for work "well done."

Enlightenment

God

Self-existent and pre-existent; not immanent; Creator, not sovereign, deism known by nature and reason

Religion

Based on study of nature and reason alone; concerned with ethics; no divine intrusion in nature

Church

University became the instituion of redemption

Science

Seeking the logic of facts; controlling principle the laws inherent in nature

Government

A government of laws, a republic vs. democracy, certain abiding laws stood above popular will

Law

Natural law, laws planted in universe by nature's Architect, derived from study of nature and nations

Nature

Created by God, but not a sphere of God's present activity; nature contains the Creator's natural laws

Life

Life can be improved without supernatural aid by natural means

The Arts

Reflect internest in the rational order of things, exemplified in neoclassical music

Work

Work becomes depersonalized service to economic order; eternal reward in doubt

Modern Secularism

God

Not self-existent or pre-existent; not transcendent but immanent; no absolute truth; possibliy nonexistent

Religion

Agnostic; private only; no propositional truth; irrational leap of faith; ethics subjective

Church

State is the instituion of redemption, but no concern for eternal value

Science

Cut of from transcendental realm, science as a means of technological manipulation; pragmatic only

Government

Progressing toward statism, wherein the state solves all problems from cradle to grave

Law

No absolute truths, only preferences relativism; legislation by special interest

Nature

Alienation; no natural order perceived, hence nature is our enemy (modern environmental concerns)

Life

Insignificant origins, therefore life is futile; no exit from time to eternity

The Arts

Chaotic, sensual, dissonant; communicating the meaninglessness of life

Work

Pragmatic; short-range goals; immediate gratification; no expectation of long-range rewards *   Chart 2

*"Battle for Our Minds: Worldviews in Collision, Study Guide," written by William H. McDowell with R.C. Sproul, Jr., Ligonier Ministries, Orlando, Florida 1992, pg. 36

Chart 1
CHRISTIAN WORLD-VIEW
What we believe...

About Individuals and Families

Rights of the unborn child • Heterosexuality in marriage; chastity outside marriage • Sex as an expression of God-given love between husband and wife • Parental responsibility • Inherent sinfulness of human nature

About Life and God

Centrality of God • Jesus Christ as perfect God—perfect man, Lord and Savior • Based on the Bible • Submissive to God's law • Freedom as a gift of God • Free will and moral accountability • Fundamental purpose to please God • Supernaturalistic

About Education

Wisdom produced by reverence for God • Truth revealed by God's Word • Parental responsibility for nurturing child's faith • Human potential fully realized only through relationship with God • Importance of Christianity in history, arts and science

About World Conditions

Man's fall underlies humansuffering • All human authority subject to God • Righteous living strengthens nations • Christian compassion as the solution to poverty • God's eventual rule of earth

About Politics

Governments instituted and upheld by God • Biblical absolutes as the ultimate test of good government • Fixed standards of morality • Checks and balances • Religion impacts all life

About Justice

Victim's rights • Evil to be punished • Protection of religious freedom • Support for traditional values and family life • Restoration of biblical standards

About Business

Compassionate use of wealth as God's gift • Ethical conduct based on biblical principles • Alliances based on preserving godly character

About Science

Orderly universe created by a personal God • Moral responsibilty of scientists for discoveries • Biblical truth as the final test of scientific theory • World problems exceed ability of science to cure • Man as spirit, soul, and body

About Eternity

God sets bounds of earthly life • God is the final judge • Eternal punishment and reward await mankind

HUMANIST WORLD-VIEW
What They believe...

About Individuals and Families

Abortion on demand • Sexual freedom; alternative lifestyles • Sex as a biological need which must be gratified; hedonism • legalized prostitution • Children's right to act independent of parents • Fundamental "goodness" of mankind

About Life and God

Centrality of man • Jesus Christ, a moral teacher, a fanatic; or a hoax • Based on Human reason • Submissive to none, except societal trends • Freedom as a human force, a matter of power • Man as a product of society's conditioning • Fundamental purpose to please self • Naturalistic

About Education

No place for God in the classroom • Truth relative according to man's circumstance • Religion not to be imposed upon children • Self-actualization; the result of education • Christianity of little importance in daily life and repressive to intellectual pursuits

About World Conditions

Human suffering disproves loving God • World leaders chart our destinies • Natural strength produced by wealth and might • Government programs as the poor's only hope • World government without God

About Politics

Governments based on cultures, economies and power • Political action based on control, consensus, and expediency • End justifies means • Checks and balances as contest for political clout • Religion has no place in public affairs

About Justice

Protection of the criminal • No evil, just need for rehabilitation • Biased decisions to restrict religious freedoms • Support of non-traditional values dissolution of family—secularization

About Business

Self-centered accumulation of wealth; materialism • Existential morality; situation ethics • Trade based on financial aspect only

About Science

Evolutionary, random world • Intellectual freedom without moral restraint • Bible is a collection of myths and fables • Science can engineer a perfect world • Man as a machine

About Eternity

Man has the right to determine his time of death • Man is his own judge • Death ends human existence, or life is a cycle of death and rebirth (reincarnation)**

**Article on "Liberation Theology Adopts Marxism" by Lester DeKoster, chart prepared by Raneld A. Hunsicker Magazine pg 16, Family Protection Scoreboard, published by National Citizens Action Network, copyright 1989, Costa Mesa, California

Many philosophers have contributed to the rise of Antinomianism. It will be the purpose of the next chapter to study the development of Antinomianism.

Discussion Questions

1. How does our worldview affect our decision making and our actions?

2. How does succumbing to Secularism affect the Christian life and mind?

3. Review the Christian worldview and the secularist worldview.

   A. What are the significant differences?

   B. What is the end result?

   C. Can these two worldviews be intermarried?

Chapter 3

Antinomian View of Ethics

Antinomianism

The term *Antinomianism* is made up of two Greek words: *anti,* meaning "against" and *nomos,* "law." An antinomian is defined as

> ...one who desires to be free from the regulations and laws of a society. He wants to live either outside society in a state of nature (like the cynics) or within society but adhering to as few social norms as possible. In theology an antinomian is (not only) one who believes that faith alone, not moral law, is necessary for salvation (but) in a stronger theological sense, he is one who despises and holds himself above all laws and

social restrictions because of some special faith, grace, or knowledge that makes for salvation.[1]

If an antinomian is simply defined as one who believes that faith alone, not moral law, is necessary for salvation, then by this definition true Christianity must be antinomian. However, a true antinomian is one who rejects the value of morality and law, upholding a license to sin. Biblical Christianity recognizes the value of law, but also acknowledges that faith alone can bring about salvation.

Antinomianism is peculiarly a religious phenomenon in which what morally would be called wrong acts are justified religiously or theologically. Professing Christians have done this on a number of grounds: by denying creation, by abasement and corruption of moral values, by biological or psychological special pleading, by dispensational rationalism, and the traditional form of antinomianism which is to misinterpret Paul's emphasis on grace in contrast to law.[2]

"Perhaps no phase of the study of Christian ethics is shrouded with such confusion today as the treatment of the Law in its relations to the Gospel."[3]

---

1. Peter A. Angeles, *Dictionary of Philosophy* (New York, New York: Harper Perennial, 1991), p. 13.
2. R.K. Harrison, ed., *Encyclopedia of Biblical and Christian Ethics* (Nashville, Tennessee: Thomas Nelson Publishers, 1987), pp. 18-19.
3. Carl F.H. Henry, *Christian Personal Ethics* (Grand Rapids, Michigan: Wm. B. Eerdmans Publishing Co., 1957), p. 350.

A balanced statement of Christian ethics must avoid the distortion of both law and gospel, protecting the former from the perversion of legalism and guarding the latter from the perversion of antinomianism.

A balanced statement of Christian ethics must avoid the distortion of both law and gospel, protecting the former from the perversion of legalism and guarding the latter from the perversion of Antinomianism.

Taken in the right sense, the law ministers to grace, and grace to the law.[4]

If the risky antinomian view is held that because the believer is saved by grace, he is free of all responsibility to law, then any proclamation of moral laws must of necessity be legalistic and antigrace. But such a view of the Christian's relationship to law does not fit the teachings of Scripture and is out of accord with the historic Christian consciousness. It is one thing to say— as indeed every Christian must—that the law as an unpaid debt-bill has been paid up in full by the mediatorial work of Christ; it is another thing to say—what Christian ethics in its best expression has deplored—that the biblically revealed moral law no longer has an instructive value for the believer.[5]

---

4.   Ibid. p. 354.
5.   Ibid. p. 288.

Identification and rejection of antinomianism by
Christians require a clear sense of the Gospel as
to what are grace, faith, justification, and
morality. Paul insists that salvation is received
by faith alone and that good works must spring
from faith. James insists the faith which justifies must be authenticated by good works. In
other words, believe and behave. ...

Most Christians have succumbed to antinomianism to varying degrees at various times, and
most churches have been tested by such views.
Modern Christians are particularly vulnerable
in view of the prevalent behavioral view of man
that morals are merely functions of mores—that
human beings are no more than behaviorally
responding organisms whose bodily functions
are no more and no less moral than the more of
the community....

Christians believe that morality is grounded in
the righteousness of God, not in situational
ethics in which every person does what appears
to be right in his own eyes. Christian morality is
more than an expression of feeling. Thus Christians teach each other to avoid evil and to do
good as an expression of the life of grace.[6]

Contrary to popular opinion and religious legalism,
the Word of God does not remove the freedom of
choice; it strengthens it. Those who advocate the

6.   Harrison, op. cit. p. 19.

freedom to do whatever they want devalue decision making. The freedom to choose anything at any time renders choice meaningless, because it strips from decision making any sense of commitment. ...True freedom is as liberating as it is limiting. It is the freedom to choose righteousness and holiness. ...Our moral decisions matter because they matter to God and determine the direction of our lives.[7]

Contrary to popular opinion and religious legalism, the Word of God does not remove the freedom of choice; it strengthens it.

In order to understand the development of Antinomianism it is necessary to consider the philosophies from the ancient world which have contributed to our present contemporary world.

Antinomianism in the Ancient World

"Ethical antinomianism has a long history. There were at least three movements in the ancient world that influenced the rise of antinomianism: processism, hedonism, and skepticism."[8]

Processism

The Greek philosopher Heraclitus of Ephesus was one of the first philosophers to use the concept of

---

7.   Taken from the book, CHOICES OF THE HEART by Douglas D. Webster, pp. 14-15. Copyright © by Douglas Webster. Used by permission of Zondervan Publishing House.
8.   Norman L. Geisler, *Christian Ethics: Options and Issues* Grand Rapids, Michigan: Baker Book House 1990, p. 29.

change as the foundation of his philosophy: Unending *flux* is the most fundamental characteristic of the universe. He is famous for saying: "All things change (flow, separate, dissolve)." "Nothing remains the same." "You cannot step into the same river twice."[9]

The Greek philosopher Cratylus (a younger contemporary of Socrates) took Heraclitus' view one step further. Cratylus extended Heraclitus' saying that everything is in constant change and no one can step into the same river twice by his contention that no one steps into the same river once. His argument was that not only was the river changing to prevent us from stepping into the same river a second time, but we also are changing during the time it takes us to attempt to step into the river the first time. "So convinced was Cratylus that all was in flux that he was not even sure that he existed. When asked about his existence, he would simply wiggle his finger, indicating that he too was in flux."[10] When we extend this kind of thinking to the realm of ethics it is clear that there can be no abiding moral laws. Since everything is changing, every ethical value will also change with the situation.

When we extend this kind of thinking to the realm of ethics it is clear that there can be no abiding moral laws. Since everything is changing, every ethical value will also change with the situation.

---

9.   Angeles, op. cit. p. 37.
10. Geisler, op. cit. p. 30.

Two points can be made in response to the view, springing from Heraclitus, that all is in flux. First Heraclitus Himself did not believe that everything is relative. In fact, he held that there was an unchanging logos beneath all change by which change could be measured. He saw this as an absolute law by which all men should live. Second, if one carries the idea of change all the way, as Cratylus tried, then he uses change to destroy change. For if everything is changing and nothing is constant, then there is no way to measure the change. Everything cannot be changing or we would not be able to know it.[11]

Hedonism

We began the discussion of hedonism when ex amining the philosophy of "what brings pleasure is right." The term *hedonism*...

> ...is derived directly from the Greek word *hedone*, which actually occurs only three times in the Greek New Testament (Lk. 8:14; Tit. 3:3; 2 Pet. 2:13) in a plural form and once (2 Pet. 2:13) in the singular. In all these occurrences it has the basic meaning of "sweetness," "pleasure," "enjoyment." Hedonism therefore is the dogma that pleasure is the principal good in human life. What is generally meant by pleasure is the delight, gratification, or enjoyment that results from indulgence in any one of a wide range of activities that give emotional satisfaction. ...But

---

11.   Geisler, op. cit. pp. 35-36.

hedonism can also exhibit a pronounced sensual aspect in which self-indulgence in food, drink, and lascivious behavior play an important part. ...From the nature of the term it is evident that the basic hedonistic concepts were shaped by Greek culture. The germ of hedonism appears among the Sophists of Plato's time, but the movement came to full flower among the Cyrenaics.[12]

The Cyrenaics believed that the highest good in life is obtaining pleasure for oneself—intense pleasure for the moment, regardless of any consequent pain. Live for present pleasures; there may not be any future. Pleasure is not only good and desirable for its own sake. Pleasure is the only criterion for deciding right and wrong. Intense, immediate physical pleasure is the best. Manipulate anything and anyone by shrewdness, intelligence, and wit in order to secure these intense pleasures. All things—wealth, power, fame, luxury—are not good in themselves or desirable in themselves but are for the attainment of pleasure.[13]

Drunkenness, lechery, and homosexuality were prominent features of Greek life, and for the egotistical hedonists constituted the main content of pleasure. The Cyrenaics were explicit exponents of this gross, sensual way of life and were followed to a more moderate extent by the Epicureans. ...With this background in view, it

---

12.   Harrison, op. cit. p. 175.
13.   Angeles, op. cit. p. 53.

is a small wonder that the New Testament condemned the love of pleasure (2 Tim. 3:4; Tit. 3:3; 2 Pet. 2:13) as a gross indulgence which would result in spiritual death (1 Tim. 5:6). Instead of partaking in worldly enjoyments even to a moderate degree, the Christian is commanded to follow the self-denying life of Jesus Christ (Mk. 8:34), to forswear luxury and personal indulgence, and to live a life of sacrifice in the faith of Christ and in service to others.[14]

2 Timothy 3:1-5: But know this, that in the last days perilous times will come: For men will be lovers of themselves, lovers of money, boasters, proud, blasphemers, disobedient to parents, unthankful, unholy, unloving, unforgiving, slanderers, without self-control, brutal, despisers of good, traitors, headstrong, haughty, lovers of pleasure rather than lovers of God, having a form of godliness but denying its power.

In response to the claims of hedonism we must list several criticisms. Applied to the realm of ethics and morals, this view contends that what is morally good for one person may be evil for another.

First of all, not all pleasures are good. For example, the sadistic pleasure some deranged individuals get from torturing little children is not good; in fact, it is grossly evil. *Second, not all pain is bad.* Pains that warn of impending disease

---

14.   Harrison, op. cit. pp. 175-176.

or damage, for instance, are good pains. *Third, it is a confusion of categories to reduce good to a pleasure.* A person is not virtuous because he is feeling good, nor is he necessarily sinful because he is suffering pain. *Finally, personal happiness may be related to happenings, but values are not.* Many martyrs have suffered adversely for their values. Hence the good cannot be equated with the pleasurable.[15]

Skepticism

Skepticism...

...comes from a Greek word *skeptomai*, "to examine, to look carefully at," and in philosophy and ethics properly denotes a questioning attitude with regard to such matters as epistomology or religious tenets. In its developed form, however, skepticism becomes a subjective, rather dogmatic rejection of traditional ethical or moral principles which often does not even admit the possibility of doubt about the validity of its own position.[16]

Skepticism is defined as "a state of doubting; a state of suspension of judgment; a state of unbelief or nonbelief. Skepticism ranges from complete, total disbelief in everything, to a tentative doubt in a process of reaching certainty.[17] Philosophical skepticism developed in Greece about the sixth century B.C. and

---

15.   Geisler, op. cit. p. 36.
16.   Harrison, op. cit. p 385.
17.   Angeles, op. cit. p. 258.

continued in various forms into the Christian period.
Some of the Greek philosophers of the ancient world
were Sextus Empiricus, Cratylus, Carneades, and Gor-
gias. Philosophers belonging to the modern period in-
clude Hume, Descartes, Kant, Locke; continuing in
various ways are the likes of Nietzsche, Dewey, and
Russell. "The skeptics insist that every issue has two
sides and every question can be argued to a stalemate.
...In ethics this would mean that nothing should ever
be considered absolutely right or wrong."[18]

> There are numerous problems with skepticism.
> First, consistent skepticism is self-defeating. If
> the skeptic were really skeptical about every-
> thing, then he would be skeptical about skep-
> ticism. If he does not doubt his doubting, then he
> is really not a skeptic but is dogmatic and wants
> to suspend judgment on everything except his
> skeptical views. Second, some things ought not
> to be doubted. Why, for example, should I doubt
> my own existence? Some things are obvious, and
> it is frivolous to deny the obvious. Third, ethics
> has to do with the way we live, but no skeptic
> can consistently live in skepticism. He cannot
> suspend judgment on whether he needs food or
> water—at least not for long. And if he is mar-
> ried, he dare not suspend judgment on whether
> he loves his wife!

> The New Testament encourages the believer to
> honor God with the mind as well as the heart
> (Mt. 22:37), implying that a critical evaluation of

18.   Geisler, op. cit. p. 30.

people and phases of thought is a legitimate and
important activity of the Christ-centered life
(1 Tim. 6:3-5). The believer must not be tossed to
and fro by false doctrine (Eph. 4:14), but must
proclaim the truth in love, confident that the
Gospel message is true (1 Thess. 2:13) and worthy of human acceptance in faith (1 Tim. 1:15).[19]

Summary of Antinomianism
in the Ancient World

		Common contributions to antinomianism
Processism	**Change** Foundation of philosophy	No abiding moral laws
		No absolutes
Hedonism	**Pleasure** Foundation of philosophy	Relativism
		Rejection of traditional ethical and moral principles
Skepticism	**Unbelief** Foundation of philosophy	

Antinomianism in the Medieval World

"Although the medieval Western world was dominated
by the Christian point of view, it still generated several

---

19.   Harrison, op. cit. p. 385.

strains of thought that contributed to antinomianism. The most notable among these were intentionalism, voluntarism, and nominalism."[20]

Intentionalism

Intentionalism is defined as "the view that the essential and defining characteristic of consciousness is: that it is able to have (understand) meanings (intention) and that it is able to direct itself conatively by intending."[21] "In the twelfth century, Peter Abelard (1) argued that an act is right if it is done with good intention and wrong if done with bad intention."[22]

> **Intentionalism is defined as the view that the essential and defining characteristic of consciousness is: that it is able to have (understand) meanings (intention) and that it is able to direct itself conatively by intending.**

This being the case, one cannot just view the act since it is not the act that is right or wrong, just the motive or intent. This causes rightness and wrongness to be relative according to the person's intentions.

Perhaps the easiest way to state the fundamental objection to intentionalism is to point out that "the road to hell is paved with good intentions." Furthermore, even Hitler had what he considered to be good intentions for the Holocaust; he wanted to weed out "inferior" strains of

---

20. Geisler, op. cit. p. 30.
21. Angeles, op. cit. p. 136.
22. Geisler, op. cit.

the human species. In addition, intentionalism wrongly assumed that because bad intentions are always bad, good intentions are always good. Bad intentions are always bad, even if they do not result in bad actions. Attempting to kill an innocent person is of course bad, even if the attempt does not succeed. However, killing handicapped people to alleviate the financial burden on society is not good no matter how noble the intention may be.[23]

As believers, we can understand the conflict that occurs with our practice and our intentions. The apostle Paul explained this struggle in Romans 7:15-25; however, we are called to walk a spiritual walk that overcomes our carnal desires (intentions) and is transformed according to the law of the Spirit of life that is found in Christ Jesus (see Rom. 8:2).

Voluntarism

Voluntarism is the belief that...

...The human will is the fundamental and ultimate ground in the making of moral decisions and in arriving at moral values. The will is superior to, and must govern the other criteria for, sources of moral worth such as conscience, the rational faculty, intuition, tradition, the feelings.[24]

The philosophical term "voluntarism" originated from the Latin *voluntas,* meaning "will, choice, inclination." Voluntarism thus describes the

---

23.   Ibid. pp. 36-37.
24.   Angeles, op. cit. p. 315.

philosophical theory which exalts the exercise of the human will over the deliberations of reason. Many ethicists trace voluntarism back to the Sophists and their disputes with Plato as he endeavored to base human action upon rational thought and decisions.[25]

The fourteenth-century thinker William of Ockham (2) argued that all moral principles are traceable to God's will. Thus God could have decided differently about what is right or what is wrong. Ockham believed that something is right because God wills it; God does not will it because it is right. If this is so, then what is morally right today may not be so tomorrow. Although Christian voluntarists took comfort in the belief that God would not change His will on basic moral issues, they could not be sure that morals would not change. In this way voluntarism helped pave the way for antinomianism.[26]

Contrary to voluntarism, an act is not good simply because God wills it. First of all, this would make God arbitrary and not essentially good. Second, it exalts God's will above His nature and allows it to operate independent of His nature. This is questionable theology at best. Third, voluntarism provides no security that God will remain constant in His ethical concerns, since He could change His mind at any time and will that hate is right rather than love.

25.   Harrison, op. cit. p. 433.
26.   Geisler, op. cit. pp. 30-31.

Fourth, an act is not good simply because it flows from the choice of the sovereign being. As we all know, sovereigns can be capricious about their will. Something is not good simply because someone else has the power to perform it. In order for it to be a good act, it must come from a good power. A will alone is not sufficient basis for good; it must be a good will.[27]

Nominalism

Nominalism is defined as...

...1. The theory that things do not have essences. 2. Definitions, and languages in general, do not refer to things but deal with the names (terms) we attach to things. 3. All universal terms, such as those indicating genus/species distinctives, and all general collective terms are only fictional names (artificial and arbitrary symbols) and have no objective, real existences that correspond to them. 4. Only particular existents (particulars) exist. Abstractions, universals, ideas, essence are only products of our language and/or of how our mind understands reality. They do not communicate what reality is like. 5. Abstractions such as "human" (a) are merely names that can be used to refer to more than one particular, (b) [and they] have no objective existence as an entity "human" or "humanhood" shared by all particular humans, and (c) cannot even be present

---

27. Ibid. p. 37.

in consciousness as an abstract idea or concept of "human," "humanhood."[28]

Nominalists believe that there are no universals.

Universals exist only in the mind, not in reality. The real world is radically individual. ...It is not difficult to see that if the same reasoning is applied to ethics, then there is no such thing as goodness or justice. There are only individual acts of justice that differ from others, but no such thing as justice itself.[29]

If nominalists are correct in saying there is no universal form or essence of meaning, then meaning could not be translated from one language to another. But translation of meaning from language to language occurs daily around the world. Thus there must be some universal basis for meaning that transcends any given language. Second, when applied to ethics this means that all good acts must participate in some universal goodness by which they are designated good acts. So there must be some universal good that is common to all good acts. Third, for the Christian this universal good is the moral character of God. To deny that God has such a transcendently good nature that it is the basis of all creaturely good is contrary to the Christian view of God.[30]

---

28.   Angeles, op. cit. p. 189.
29.   Geisler, op. cit. p. 31.
30.   Ibid. p. 37.

Summary of Antinomianism
in the Medieval World

Antinomianism in the Modern World

Intentionalism	Motive or Intent define "right"	Common Contributions to Antinomianism
		No abiding moral laws
		No absolutes
Voluntarism	Human Will Ground in making moral decisions	Relativism
		Radical individualism
Nominalism	Universals exist only in the mind not in reality	No universals
		Individual motive, intent, will and acts of justice

"The growth of relativism in the modern world is manifest in three movements: utilitarianism, existentialism, and evolutionism. Each of these contributes in its own way to antinomianism."[31]

Utilitarianism

Utilitarianism is the revival in modern times of the pleasure principle which ancient Cyrenaic and Epicurean ethics projected unsuccessfully as the rule of life. ...The supreme rule of life for Utilitarianism is neither the short-term nor the long-term pleasure of any individual as such,

---

31.   Ibid.

but rather the greatest happiness of the greatest number of people. If the Cyrenaic formula is the pleasure for the moment, and the Epicurean the pleasure of a life, the Utilitarian is the maximal earthly pleasure of all lives.[32]

Utilitarianism took its formation from Jeremy Bentham (1748-1832) [3] and James Mill.

The supreme rule of life for Utilitarianism is neither the short-term nor the long-term pleasure of any individual as such, but rather the greatest happiness of the greatest number of people.

The son of the latter, John Stuart Mill (1806-1873),[4], gave the theory its traditional definition in his 1851 essay *Utilitarianism: "The creed which accepts as the foundation of morals utility, or the greatest happiness principle, holds that actions are right in proportion as they tend to promote happiness, wrong as they tend to produce the reverse of happiness. By 'happiness' is intended pleasure, and the absence of pain; by 'unhappiness,' pain, and the privation of pleasure."* Ever since, the popular short definition of Utilitarianism has been the doctrine that the greatest happiness of the greatest number should be the guiding principle of action.[33]

John Stuart Mill understood the utilitarian calculus in a qualitative sense.

---

32. Henry, op. cit. p. 37
33. Harrison, op. cit. p. 421.

He believed that some pleasures were of higher quality than others. He went so far as to say it would be better to be an unhappy man than a happy pig, for the intellectual and aesthetic qualities of human life are qualitatively superior to the mere physical pleasures of an animal. In any event there are no absolute moral laws.[34]

This doctrine of utilitarianism is results oriented. The ends justify the means. It does not matter what you do to get the results, as long as you get the results and the results serve the greatest number with pleasurable experiences. However, results alone cannot justify the action taken to accomplish the intended purpose. Utilitarians take the end to be a universal good, showing that they cannot avoid the concept that there must be some universal good. So even here there must be some standard outside the desires by which good is measured even if that good is being defined by the recipients of the actions taken.

Existentialism

"Basically a twentieth-century movement, existentialism has its roots in the nineteenth century with such figures as Soren Kierkegaard (1813-1855)[5]and Friedrich Nietzsche (1844-1900)[6]. But it is in the present century that existentialism made its impact on the intellectual world."[35]

Some of the following themes are common to existentialists: First, existence precedes essence.

---

34. Geisler, op. cit. p. 31.
35. Harrison, op. cit. p. 141.

Forms do not determine existence to be what it is. Existence fortuitously becomes and is whatever it becomes and is, and that existence then makes up its "essence." Second, an individual has no essential nature, no self-identity other than that involved in the act of choosing. Third, truth is subjective. Fourth, abstractions can never grasp nor communicate the reality of individual existence. Fifth, philosophy must concern itself with the human predicament and inner states such as alienation, anxiety, inauthenticity, dread, sense of nothingness, anticipation of death. Sixth, the universe has no rational direction or scheme. It is meaningless and absurd. Seventh, the universe does not provide moral rules. Moral principles are constructed by humans in the context of being responsible for their actions and for the actions of others. Eighth, individual actions are unpredictable. Ninth, individuals have complete freedom of the will. Tenth, individuals cannot help but make choices. Eleventh, an individual can become completely other that what he is.[36]

Some of the following themes are common to existentialists:

1. Existence precedes essence.

2. An individual has no essential nature, no self-identity other than that involved in the act of choosing.

36. Angeles, op. cit. p. 88.

3. Truth is subjective.

4. Abstractions can never grasp nor communicate the reality of individual existence.

5. Philosophy must concern itself with the human predicament and inner states such as alienation, anxiety, inauthenticity, dread, sense of nothingness, anticipation of death.

6. The universe has no rational direction or scheme. It is meaningless and absurd.

7. The universe does not provide moral rules. Moral principles are constructed by humans in the context of being responsible for their actions of others.

8. Individual actions are unpredictable.

9. Individuals have complete freedom of the will.

10. Individuals cannot help but make choices.

11. An individual can become completely other than what he is.

The rise of existentialism corresponds with an altered consciousness that was precipitated by the tragedy of the First World War. This new outlook involved the disenchantment with the hitherto prevailing optimism, a deepening appreciation of the tragedy of human condition, and a growing conviction that reason was inadequate to serve as a guide to life. In this congenial environment, existentialism made its inroads among both humanists and religious philosophers, including such figures as Jean-Paul Sartre (1905-1980)[7], Jacques Maritain (1882-1973), Gabriel Marcel (1889-1973), Karl Jaspers (1883-1969), and Martin Heidegger (1889-1976).

All these writers endorsed a radical sense of freedom. What am I to be? What am I to live for? What am I to do with my existence? What values shall I affirm? There was seen to be no rationally correct answer to these questions. Rather the individual is free to select any answer without fear of contradiction by reason. Thus there is a freedom from radical determinism.[37]

In responding to existentialism, many criticisms can be stated:

First, if everyone literally "did their own thing," it would be chaos, which would hinder anyone from doing his own "thing." Second, even free choices need a context or structure. Absolute freedom for two or more persons is impossible, for if one person chooses to do to others what they choose not to have done to them, then an unavoidable conflict emerges. That is why law is necessary to structure free choice, thus maximizing the freedom of all without negating the freedom of any. Third, no free act is without justification; otherwise one is unjustified in performing it. No action escapes the first principle

---

37. Harrison, op. cit. p. 141.

of justice any more than a thought can escape the first principle of noncontradiction. Both thought and action are justified by first principles, and he who breaks first principles will in the end be broken by first principles.[38]

Evolutionism

Evolutionism is the general name given to developmental views of life or the universe. Charles Darwin [8] believed in a process of natural selection in nature that brings about the survival of the fittest in a struggle for existence. This theory applied to society is known as social Darwinism. It is the...

...theory that society is a state of struggle for existence in which the fittest (strongest) wins. The strongest is characterized by egoism, ruthlessness, competition, ambition, manipulation, scheming, intelligence, energy, wealth, power. "Might makes right." Social selection operates in society much the same way as natural selection operates in nature, whereby the unfit (weakest) is eliminated.

Social Darwinism is the theory that society is in a state of struggle for existence in which the fittest (strongest) wins.

The unfit are characterized as being noncompetitive, altruistic, idle, lazy, powerless, poor. The good of society as a whole is served in this social struggle for existence.[39]

---

38.   Geisler, op. cit. p. 39.

After Darwin, men like Herbert Spencer (1820-1903) expanded evolution into cosmic theory. Others, such as T.H. Huxley (1825-1895) and Julian Huxley (1887-1975), worked out an evolutionary ethic. The central tenet is that whatever aids the evolutionary process is right and whatever hinders it is wrong. Julian Huxley laid down three principles of evolutionary ethics: it is right to realize ever-new possibilities in evolution; it is right to respect human individuality and to encourage its fullest development; it is right to construct a mechanism for future social evolution.[40]

Biologist Julian Huxley devoted most of his life to integrating evolution and the humanist worldview.

Julian Huxley laid down three principles of evolutionary ethics.
  1. It is right to realize ever-new possibilities in evolution.
  2. It is right to respect human individuality and to encourage its fullest development.
  3. It is right to construct a mechanism for future social evolution.

He states the following:

I use the word "Humanist" to mean someone who believes that man is just as much a natural phenomenon as an animal or a plant, that his body, his mind, and his soul were not supernaturally

---

39.   Angeles, op. cit. p. 54.
40.   Geisler, op. cit. p. 32.

created but are all products of evolution, and that he is not under the control or guidance of any supernatural Being or beings, but has to rely on himself and his own powers.[41]

Belief in evolutionary theory would require more faith than belief in creationism, since evolution runs contrary to reason. Still many evolutionists hold desperately to their theory, simply because it is the only explanation of origins that excludes God. The scientist who believes that everything can be explained in natural terms cannot tolerate the concept of a supernatural Being.

Biologist Julian Huxley devoted most of his life to integrating evolution and the humanist worldview. He states, "I use the word 'Humanist' to mean someone who believes that man is just as much a natural phenomenon as an animal or a plant, that his body, his mind, and his soul were not supernaturally created but are all products of evolution, and that he is not under the control or guidance of any supernatural Being or beings, but has to rely on himself and his own powers."

But for the Christian biologist, the world is only comprehensible in light of God's existence. This is especially true when one considers the question of origins. Robert Jastrow accurately summarizes

41.   Julian Huxley, in Roger E. Greeley, ed., *The Best of Humanism* with Roger E. Greeley, ed., (Buffalo: Prometheus Books, 1988), pp. 194-195.

the clash between the materialistic scientist and the Christian with regard to origins:[42]

At this moment it seems as though science will never be able to raise the curtain on the mystery of creation. For the scientist who has lived by his faith in the power of reason, the story ends like a bad dream. He has scaled the mountains of ignorance; he is about to conquer the highest peak; as he pulls himself over the final rock, he is greeted by a band of theologians who have been sitting there for centuries.[43]

The point, however, is that the doctrine of evolution has swept the world, not on the strength of its scientific merits, but precisely in its capacity as a Gnostic myth. It affirms, in effect, that living beings create themselves, which is, in essence a metaphysical claim. This in itself implies, however, that the theory is scientifically unverifiable (a fact, incidentally, which has often enough been pointed out by philosophers of science). Thus, in the final analysis, evolutionism is in truth a metaphysical doctrine decked out in scientific garb.[44]

Perhaps we can best sum up the shaky position of evolutionism with the words written to Charles Darwin in a letter by his wife. "May not the habit in scientific

42. David A. Noebel, *Understanding the Times* (Manitou Springs, Colorado: Summit Press, 1992), p. 348.
43. Robert Jastrow, *God and the Astronomers* (New York: W.W. Norton, 1978), p. 116.
44. Wolfgang Smith, *Teilhardism and the New Religion* (Rockford, Illinois: Tan Books, 1988), p. 2.

pursuits of believing nothing till it is proved, influence your mind too much in other things which cannot be proved in the same way, and which if true, are likely to be above our comprehension?"[45]

Summary of Antinomianism in the Modern World

		Common Contributions to Antinomianism
Utilitarianism	Maximum earthly pleasure of all lives	Right is what you feel is right
	Results oriented	Ends justify means
	Ends justify means	Truth is subjective
Existentialism	Existence preceeds essence	Individual choice affirmed
	Universe is meaningless and absurd	No universal moral rules
		Survival of the fittest
Evolutionism	What aids evolutionary process is right	Humanism
	Survival of the fittest	No supernatural control or guidance
		Might makes right
		Happiness not justice for greatest number of people

---

45.   N. Barlow, *Autobiography of Charles Darwin* (London: Collins, 1958), pp. 235-237.

Antinomianism in the Contemporary World

"Several movements in the contemporary world contribute to a lawless morality. Three that stand out are emotivism, nihilism, and situationism. In their extreme forms, all of these are antinomian."[46]

Emotivism

Emotivism is a noncognitive theory:

Ethical knowledge is different from other kinds of knowledge such as factual, scientific, conceptual, cognitive, logical. Words like "right," "wrong," "bad," "good," "should," "ought to," (a) do not refer to qualities in things, (b) cannot be said to be true or false (since they do not describe any states of affairs), (c) cannot be formally deduced or demonstrated by means of logical system, and (d) cannot be empirically verified by such things as experimentation, observation, testing procedures. Ethical words function similarly to interjections ("Terrific!"), imperatives ("Do that!"), prescriptions ("Thou shalt..."), optatives ("Would that...!"), or performative utterances ("I apologize"). Ethical statements are expressions of such things as blame, praise prohibitions, derogation, used (1) to influence conduct and/or (2) to express emotions, feelings, attitudes, or (3) to evoke similar emotions. They request, exhort, command, persuade, advise, cajole. Ethical disagreement (disagreement about convictions or values) is actually disagreement about attitudes. For some emotive theorists,

---

46. Geisler p. 31.

ethical statements may indirectly be cognitive, in that they may provide information about one's attitude, beliefs, ideas, commitments, and convictions.[47]

A.J. Ayer (1910-1970) argued that all ethical statements are emotive. That is, they are really only an expression of our feeling. Thus statements like "thou shalt not kill" really mean "I dislike killing" or "I feel killing is wrong." Ethical statements are merely expostulations of our subjective feelings. There are no divine imperatives. Everything is relative to one's individual feelings. Hence, there are no objective moral laws which are binding on all persons everywhere.[48]

Nihilism

The downward course to Nihilism began in Cynicism, which was a reactionary movement caused by the revolt of Aristippus of Cyrene.

The title Cynic derived from *Kuon,* dog, which teachers of the movement adopted as a sign of their return to the simplicity of animal existence. "Return to nature" was their motto. Antisthenes (444-399 B.C.), founder of Cynicism, was called the "downright" dog; his most notable follower Diogenes (412-323 B.C.), the "royal" dog. The Cynics fixed upon the negative ascetic element as an end in itself and championed renunciation. They acknowledged nothing holy,

47. Angeles, op. cit. p. 83.
48. Geisler, op. cit. p. 32.

withdrew from society, flouted contemporary norms and human ties. Civil and social relations were regarded as impositions. Society is accident said Cynicism; man should be sufficient unto himself. ...Hippias taught that social laws and institutions are arbitrary and harmful, enslaving true human nature which is individual and specific; the good life consists in renouncing them. ...By 275 B.C. Cynicism reaped its ripe harvest of "antinomianism and quixotry".[49]

Nihilism is defined as...

...the theory that moral values cannot be justified in any way—not by reason, by a god, by intuition, by conscience, or by the authority of the state or law. Moral values are expressions of arbitrary and capricious behavior or expressions of loose feelings and reasonless, social conditioning; and they are worthless, meaningless, and irrational.[50]

Nihilism is defined as the theory that moral values cannot be justified in any way—not by reason, by a god, by intuition, by conscience, or by the authority of the state or law. Moral values are expressions of arbitrary and capricious behavior or expressions of loose feelings and reasonless, social conditioning; and they are worthless, meaningless, and irrational.

---

49. Henry, op. cit. pp. 28-29.
50. Angeles, op. cit. p. 188.

The term originated in the Latin word *nihil,* meaning "nothing." For the nihilist there can be no rational justification in religious belief for such things are metaphysical standards or norms, and therefore any objective basis for morals and ethics is totally illusory. While it may be possible for the nihilist to speak of such things as social mores, it can only be done by recognizing that they are in fact the expression of community traditions and can have no ultimate or binding authority. ... *Nihilism not unnaturally exhibits pessimism and cynicism about the prospects for individual and collective human existence. According to its adherents there can be no objective standards for morality, faith, or truth, and hence they fall victim to the misconception of the ancient Greek Sophists that everything is relative and that the individual is his or her own arbiter. ...Nihilists betray all the characteristics of those whom the psalmist reviled for dismissing the existence of God as a fact of life (Ps. 53:1). Their personal misery and sense of hopelessness is evident on all sides, and their literary musings make for very depressing reading.*[51]

The famous German atheist Friedrich Nietzsche (1844-1900) said, "God is dead and we have killed him." When God died all objective values died with him. The Russian novelist Fyodor Dostoevsky (1821-1881) noted correctly that if God is dead, then anything goes. For Nietzsche, the

---

51.   Harrison, op. cit. pp. 277-278.

death of God meant not only the death of God-
given values, but also the need for man to create
his own values. In doing so, he argued we must
go "beyond good and evil." Since there is no God
to will what is good, we must will our own good.
And since there is no eternal value, we must will
the eternal recurrence of the same state of affairs. Nietzsche said, in the last line of *The
Geneology of Morals*, that he would rather will
nothingness than not will at all.[52]

[Apostle] Paul had encountered *de facto* nihilist
in Ephesus (the "beasts," perhaps, of 1 Cor.
15:32), and in his letter to the church there he
reminded the members of their own hopeless,
lost condition before they accepted Christ as
Savior (Eph. 2:12). Conversion to the Christian
faith is the only specific means by which new life
and lasting hope for the future can be assured,
both for the nihilist and anyone else. This occurs
through the renewing of the mind (Rom. 12:2),
which transforms the unregenerate, lost nature
and gives it an eternal dimension based on the
saving work of Christ. He alone is the hope of
mankind, and the very antithesis of nihilism,
being in fact the fulness of God Himself (Eph.
1:23; Col. 1:19). The Christian life, therefore, is
one of hope and joyous expectation of a future
existence with Christ, in stark contrast to that
of a nihilist, which, ironically enough, will be
reduced to nothingness at the final assessment
of human values.[53]

---

52.   Geisler, op. cit. pp. 32-33.

> The Christian life, therefore, is one of hope
> and joyous expectation of a future existence
> with Christ, in stark contrast to that of a
> nihilist, which, ironically enough, will be
> reduced to nothingness at the final assess-
> ment of human values.

Situationism

According to this view, everything is relative to
the situation in which one finds oneself. Although the contemporary ethicist Joseph
Fletcher claims to believe in one absolute ethical
norm, he has no absolute moral principles with
substantive content. In this sense, his view contributes heavily to antinomianism. Fletcher
says we should avoid words such as "never" and
"always." There are no moral principles that
apply to all people at all times. All ethical
decisions are expedient and circumstantial.[54]

The ethical position known as situational ethics
arose in the 1960s as a radical response to a view
that saw Christian ethics chiefly in terms of rule-
keeping. Situational ethics emphasized three
things: the overwhelming value in Christian ethics
of self-giving love (*agape*); the need for Christians
to be autonomous in their moral reasoning and to
come to moral judgments as the result of free-
decision; and the solidity of the moral life. In

---

53.   Harrison, op. cit. p. 278.
54.   Geisler, op. cit. p. 33.

the last of these emphases, situational ethics is undoubtedly influenced by existentialism, which stresses the importance of individual choice and the idea that no person can know beforehand what ethical demands a particular situation may make upon him. ...The slogan "people before principles" is an apt summary of the position of the individual and of the moral judgment he is to make of situations. ...the basic assumption of situational ethics, that law and love are opposites, is not one that can be supported from the Bible, where love is the content of the divine law (Mt. 22:36-40) and is said to be the fulfilling of that law (Rom. 13:10), and where unlawful behavior is unequivocally condemned. The Bible also stresses that the observation of the law of God is not to be legalistic, that is, concerned with minor matters at the expense of the major, nor blind to the possible conflicts of laws in the daily living of life, such as situations in which the lesser of two evils ought to be followed. But situational ethics appears to pay scant regard either to the real nature of ethical conflict or to the depths and subleties of the development of moral character.[55]

Situational ethics emphasized three things:

1. The overwhelming value in Christian ethics of self-giving love (*agape*).

---

55. Harrision, op. cit. p. 384.

2. **The need for Christians to be autonomous in their moral reasoning and to come to moral judgments as the result of free-decision.**

3. **The solidity of the moral life.**

Summary of the Antinomianism in the Contemporary World

		Common Contributions to Antinomianism
Emotivism	No divine imperatives	No divine imperatives
	Everything—relative to one's individual feelings	No objective moral laws
		Nothing holy
Nihilism	Return to nature	Man is sufficient
	Nothing holy	No ultimate or binding authority
	Man sufficient unto himself	No objective standards
Situationism	Relative to situation	No absolute moral principles
	People before principles	Everything is relative
	No absolute moral principles	Individual choice
		Feelings rule over any standard
		Man creates own values

Antionomianism and Christianity

Developmentally, Antinomianism has been expressed in many diverse forms. Antinomianism can be classified in two general groups, "outright" and "latent." The outright antinomian is one who sees any form of external authority as a threat to his freedom. The basic beliefs of this antinomian can be stated as there are no "God-given moral laws," "objective moral laws," "timeless moral laws," or "laws against laws." In other words, these antinomians are either theoretical or practical atheists, who refuse to accept that there are more than subjective choices to be made relative to the individual. They believe that morals are simply mores, and they change from place to place and time to time. Ultimately, they are not only against law, they are without law, "lawless."

Critically speaking, Antinomianism is self-defeating, too subjective, too individualistic, ineffective, and irrational. There is no way to be a consistent relativist; there must be some standard from which to begin, some starting line. The antinomian is not only playing a game without rules, but he is also playing a game without umpires. Thus, it can be no more than a free-for-all in which anything goes. Moral conflicts cannot be resolved since there are no unifying standards. All views cannot possibly be true. Outright antinomianism is just a radical form of ethical relativism denying all valid ethical absolutes. For this individual, maintenance of the law of God would be considered legalism and living by the letter rather than living in the Spirit. He would rather replace the objective authority of God's revealed principles (law) with Christian self-determination, conscience, and "freedom."

> **Outright antinomianism is just a radical form of ethical relativism denying all valid ethical absolutes.**

"This brand of antinomianism is out of accord with what we have found God's word to teach about the law, sanctification, the Spirit, the covenant, grace and love; it is simply a non-Christian ethic baptized with Christian terminology."[56]

While outright antinomianism is not prevalent among Christians today, the latent brand of antinomianism is quite prevalent. On the surface these Christians seem to accept the principles of God's law and seem to have a concern for it, yet their attitude still feeds from the polluted stream of antinomianism. *Webster's Dictionary* defines latent as "present or potential but not evident or active;" when used as a noun, "a fingerprint that is difficult to see but can be made visible for examination." We can further define a latent in terms of "the incubation period of an infectious disease, or the interval between stimulus and response."[57] Because of this hidden philosophy, a latent

---

56. Greg L. Bahnsen, *Theonomy in Christian Ethics* (Phillipsburg, New Jersey: Presbyterian and Reformed Publishing Company, 1984), p. 307.

57. *Webster's II New Riverside University Dictionary* (Boston, Massachusetts: The Riverside Publishing Company, 1984), p. 678.

antinomian is not always known until conditions in his life cause him to make certain moral decisions. How those decisions are made determine which standard or standards he follows.

The difficulty with this ethic is that through self-directed arbitration the Christian determines which of God's laws are appropriate to his life today. He is selective in deciding which principles are applicable for the present. In the final analysis he is his own moral authority. He may honor God with his lips, but his heart is far from Him. He limits God's law as it applies to him and therefore denies the Lordship of Christ in ethics by turning the grace of God into licentiousness (see Jude 4). Rather than becoming a servant of righteousness he becomes a slave to sin (see Rom. 6:16-18). By rubber-stamping God's law only when it parallels his own feelings, he has founded his house on the sand and does not attempt to follow and do the Lord's sayings (see Lk. 6:46). This smorgasbord approach subtly does not recognize all of God's law as obligation and allows portions to be nullified without clear scriptural justification. The end reality is self-law, since submission to God's will is not a reality.

Latent Antinomianism also expresses itself through improper hermeneutical principles, either shaving off the laws of God or distinguishing between different facets of life and then declaring that Scripture applies only to matters of "faith." The apostle Paul in writing a letter to Timothy said, "All Scripture is given by inspiration of God, and is profitable for doctrine, for reproof, for correction, for instruction in righteousness, that the man of God may be complete, thoroughly equipped for every good work" (2 Tim. 3:16-17). He saw God's law as something to guide all of life. The writer of Hebrews quotes the Lord as saying, "For this is the covenant that I will make with the house of Israel after those days, says the Lord: I will put My laws in their mind and write them on their hearts; and I will be their God, and they shall be My people—(Heb. 8:10).

The writer of Proverbs taught the relationship of our heart to all of life's facets: "Keep your heart with all diligence, for out of it spring the issues of life" (Prov. 4:23). Life cannot be portioned like a house, in which walls divide its rooms and each room has a different function. One cannot apply certain principles to one area of life without affecting another. Yet many Christians, like the non-Christians, continue to compartmentalize their life so that they may continue to live their preference rather than God's principle.

When approaching the study of God's Word, this same principle has been applied. We cannot segment the flow of God's Word any more than we can segment His commands to us. Scripture is a progressive revelation. Discontinuity cannot be scripturally justified.

Many Christians, like the non-Christians, continue to compartmentalize their life so that they may continue to live their preference rather than God's principle.

Continuity was presupposed by the writers of the New Testament. New Testament apostles built upon the foundation of the Old Testament teachings (see Mt. 5:17). What was written in earlier times was written for our instruction and ongoing edification (see Rom. 15:4). The New Testament must be used to understand, not undermine, the Old Testament. The Bible is a covenantal book and must be interpreted in and through covenant. Because of continuity, commands stated in the old covenant that have not been repeated in the New Testament are not automatically annulled. Only God has the authority and prerogative to discontinue the binding force of anything He has revealed; man must live by everything which proceeds from God's mouth (see Mt. 4:4).

Another way that latent Antinomianism distorts hermeneutic principles is oversimplification. Summarizations are never a substitute for the whole. The Bible must be studied in context of the whole. All interpretations need biblical cross-references. Interpretation works from part to whole and whole to part. Scripture interprets Scripture. The New Testament gives examples of authoritative use and application of Old Testament law. Only through the whole counsel of God can we build a house that will stand (see Mt. 7:24).

Not all Christians are aware that their moral reasonings and rationalizations are subtly antinomian. As believers, we must make a careful examination of our lives. Our motives need to be reviewed, and by faith we must allow the law of God to be established in our lives (see Rom. 3:31). We must be submitted to God with a whole heart (see Mt. 6:24), remembering that the Spirit witnesses to the law and empowers our obedience.

Not all Christians are aware that their moral reasonings and rationalizations are subtly antinomian. As believers, we must make a careful examination of our lives. Our motives need to be reviewed, and by faith we must allow the law of God to be established in our lives (see Rom. 3:31). We must be submitted to God with a whole heart (see Mt. 6:24) remembering that the Spirit witnesses to the law and empowers our obedience.

Discussion Questions

1. Define Antinomianism. How might Antinomianism distort a Christian worldview?

2. Choose one or more of the movements that have contributed to Antinomianism and list both positive and negative contributions that this philosophy brought forth, and prepare an apologetic defense to the Christian faith.

3. Discuss the difference between outright and latent Antinomianism.

   A. How might latent Antinomianism be expressed?

   B. What happens when we compartmentalize our life?

Chapter 4

Christian View of Ethics

Introduction

"Ethics is in the first place a statement about God—who He is, how He acts, what He values. ...Ethical behavior is a consequence of man's becoming fully personal through the realization of his immediate relationship to the will and purpose of God."[1]

Every person who engages in moral judgment implies by his judgment the existence of an objective moral order. This is because the relationship called judging involves at least three terms:

1. G.W. Bromiley, "Philosophical Ethics: Nature and Function," *The International Standard Bible Encyclopedia* (Grand Rapids, Michigan: William B. Eerdmans Publishing Company, reprinted 1988), p. 167.

the person who judges, the action that is judged, and the standard of judgment by which the judged action is measured. This last, if moral experience is to make sense at all, must be something independent of both of the other terms.[2]

The relationship called judging involves at least three terms:

1. The person who judges.

2. The action that is judged.

3. The standard of judgment by which the judged action is measured.

"Christian Ethics goes back to God as the ultimate ground and source of morality."[3]

He is the supreme rule of right. He defines the whole content of morality by His own revealed will.

The wise man is one who sees beyond principles, rules, and other screens to the reality of God. He is the supreme rule of right.

It is not merely because "in God is the perfect realization of the Ideal Righteousness," but because God legislates the nature of the good, that biblical ethics is a radical departure from the pagan view of the moral order.[4]

2. D. Elton Trueblood, *Philosophy of Religion* (Grand Rapids, Michigan: Baker Book House, 1975), p. 111.
3. Leander S. Keyser, *A Manual of Christian Ethics* (Burlington, Iowa: The Lutheran Literary Board, 1926), p. 31.
4. George Walker, *The Idealism of Christian Ethics*, Baird Lecture, 1928 (Edinburgh: T. & T. Clark Co., 1929), p. 30.

Biblical ethics discredits an autonomous morality. ...The biblical view maintains always a dynamic statement of values, refusing to sever the elements of morality from the will of God.[5]

"The task of Christian ethics is determining what conforms to God's character and what does not."[6] *"Thus, the beginning point of Christian ethics is not rules but the form of Christ and formation of the Church in conformity with the form of Christ."*[7] *"The performance of God's will alone constitutes man's highest good."*[8] "The Apostle Paul's perspective is the same. The teaching of Romans 12:2 is that 'the good, the acceptable, the perfect is the will of God.'"[9] The conflict between duty and happiness is resolved by the grace of God at work on the heart of the believer, "for it is God who works in you both to will and to do for His good pleasure" (Phil. 2:13, NKJ).

The task of Christian ethics is determining what conforms to God's character and what does not. Thus, the beginning point of Christian ethics is not rules but the form of Christ and formation of the Church in conformity with the form of Christ. The performance of God's will alone constitutes man's highest good.

5.   Carl F.H. Henry, *Christian Personal Ethics* (Grand Rapids, Michigan: Wm. B. Eerdmans Publishing Co., 1957), p. 210.

6.   David A. Noebel, *Understanding the Times* (Manitou Spring, Colorado: Summit Press, 1992), p. 238.

7.   Dietrich Bonhoeffer, in Eberhard Bethge, ed., *Ethics* (New York: Macmillan, 1968), p. 84.

8.   W.G.D. MacLennan, *Christian Obedience* (London: Thomas Nelson and Sons Ltd., 1948), p. 100.

9.   G.C. Adolph von Harless, *System of Christian Ethics*, (Edinburgh: T. & T. Clark., 1887) p. 63.

The rule of life is to "seek first the Kingdom of God and His righteousness" (Mt. 6:33). The stress Jesus placed on the spiritual aspect of the Kingdom of God as the Rule of God in the lives of His servants reinforces this idea that the good life is submission to the sovereign God.[10]

MacLennan singles out as

the most important conception in His teaching...the living of life in whole hearted loyalty to God and unquestioning obedience to His will in this world here and now. He is urging upon men the seeing and accepting of the rule of God in their daily living. If they see and grasp that central reality of life, all else will fall into line and life will take on the power and a peace and joy which can be found no other way. ...It is clear that the Rule of God as taught by Jesus demands an obedience of nature which is nothing less than a complete subordination of the human will to the will of God. The motto for any son of the Kingdom, as for Jesus Himself, is: "Not what I will but what You will." It is a demand quite as rigorous as ever made under the law.[11]

The nature of man is to oppose law, thinking it limits his freedom. True liberty and conformity to law, however, are far from being mutually exclusive, they are in fact complementary:

10.   Henry, op. cit. pp. 217-218.
11.   MacLennan, op. cit. pp. 16,18.

It is only when man walks along the path de-
lineated by God's Commandments that he can
realize true fulfillment of his personality. The law
is not a tyrannical imposition, confining man and
cramping his opportunity to enjoy life: on the
contrary, it is God's gracious revelation of the structure of the spiritual universe, which teaches man to
move along the cosmos' lines of force rather than
at cross-purpose with his true destiny.[12]

"The will of God so reveals His character that the
man who conforms to His commandments will exhibit
the image of God in his life."[13]

*The ultimate ethical purpose is the praise of God.
God is praised as His will is done, and obedience is
the means to achieve this goal. Obedience is something
we come into through a relational experience with
God.* This relationship is based upon a divine destiny
for all of God's creation. There is flow in which this
relationship can be expressed: love that leads to fellowship that leads to service. We can further express the
ethic of relationship by the divine will, enablement,
sanction, mission, and preparation.

Divine Will—Unity

God's divine will is to bring unity to all of life.
Psalm 103:19 (NIV) says, *"The Lord has established*

---

12. Roger R. Nicole, "Authority," in Carl F.H. Henry, ed., *Baker's
Dictionary of Christian Ethics* (Grand Rapids, Michigan:
Baker Book House, 1973), p. 47.
13. Henry, op. cit. p. 213.

His throne in heaven, and His kingdom rules over all."
The word *establish* means "to make secure or firm; to
cause to be recognized and accepted; to set in a secure
condition or position."[14] The word *throne* speaks of a
sovereign rank or power, of the chair occupied by this
sovereign one. His "kingdom" is the entire realm over
which God's sovereignty extends, where He exercises
limits and restraints as He governs. Without some
form of government, lawlessness, anarchy, and chaos
result. In a larger perspective, Philippians 2:9-11 says
*that the entire universe acknowledges that Jesus
Christ is Lord to the glory of God the Father.* All existing things, including the earth and the heavens, will
confess and admit to the reality and the truth that
Jesus is Lord, bringing ultimate glory to God the
Father. It also speaks of a time when the Church,
God's instrument in the world, will come into full
realization of its ultimate destiny of growing in the
image of God, functioning in interpersonal relationships and in fellowship, until the awaiting universe
sees God in His Person revealed to redeemed men and
women—forevermore.

*Unity is attained and maintained by belief in one
God* (see Deut. 6:4). When we fail to maintain this
relationship through disobedience, we come out of
divine order only to be dominated by the one who has
rebelled among the angels of God in Heaven and was

---

14. *Webster's II New Riverside University Dictionary* (Boston,
     Massachusetts: The Riverside Publishing Company, 1984),
     p. 444.

cast down in judgment with punishment. Rebellion is an uprising or organized opposition intended to change or overthrow an existing government or ruling authority without the legal right or authority to do so. Rebellion is a problem in character which does not come under rule. The cross begins here with two opposing thoughts—self-will or God's will; rebellion or submission; self-authority or God's authority.

The fallen world of ethical rebellion is depicted in Scripture as under the sway of Satan. It is a kingdom of darkness whose creatures are the servants of the evil one. Twice Jesus speaks of the unregenerate as "children of Satan" (Mt. 13:38; Jn. 8:44). He is the spirit that works in the "children of disobedience" (Eph. 2:2). The New Testament pinpoints the background for stark realities of evil in satan himself. ...Satan is described as the god of this world, blinding the minds of the unbelieving (2 Cor. 4:3). ...Satan remains as the defiant and influential power in the world of unbelief, which is in darkness (Col. 1:13). The cosmos uncommitted to the Christ is ruled by Satan (Eph. 2:2; Mt. 4:16; Lk. 22:53; Acts 26:18; Rom. 13:12; Eph. 5:8; 6:12). But all excuse for ignorance of the real Lord of heaven and earth is removed by Christ's resurrection (Acts 17:30).[15]

Adam, God's first delegated human authority in the earth (see Gen. 1:28), was seduced along with Eve

---

15.   Henry, op. cit. pp. 175-176.

to come out from under the authority of God and thus came under divine judgment for his sin (see Gen. 3:24). We, being sons in the flesh, have this sin imputed to us and are in need of a Savior to redeem us from our bondage. God continues to rule. When Jesus prayed in Matthew 6:10, "Thy Kingdom come," He was saying may we come under God's rule and order. The manifestation of God's Kingdom on earth will be fully realized when every hostile and wicked power is judged and salvation is attained by the righteous who have been redeemed from their burden of sin and receive the benefits of the Kingdom.

When Jesus prayed in Matthew 6:10, "Thy Kingdom come," He was saying may we come under God's rule and order.

This kingship is not only something in the future, but something present (see Lk. 17:21). It is God's rule, which we must receive as little children here and now (see Mk. 10:15), not only seeking the Kingdom for the future, but in our present existence (see Mt. 6:33; Lk. 12:31). The Kingdom has actually come among us in the person and works of Jesus (see Mt. 12:28). The message of the Kingdom is "God is near." He is confronting people with the challenge to decision. In the person of Christ, all that the prophets had hoped for and predicted has been realized. God has entered into history in His kingly power to defeat the powers of evil and to bring to people a foretaste of the blessings of the eschatological Kingdom while they still live in this present age. One of the most characteristic works of Jesus was freeing people from their demonic bondage. This is a sign of the presence of the Kingdom of God. This present defeat of satan is also seen in the mission of Jesus' disciples (see Lk. 10:9,17). This mighty working of the Kingdom of God requires a mighty response—"men of violence" must "take it by force." We must be willing and ready to engage in any action, however radical, in response to the presence of the Kingdom of God.

The Book of Revelation pictures the plight of a persecuted Church in a hostile world, but assures the Church that Christ has already won a victory over the powers of evil (see Rev. 5:5) by virtue of which He can finally destroy them (see Rev. 19:11–20:14). Revelation closes with a highly symbolic picture of the Kingdom of God (see chapters 21 and 22) when God comes to dwell among His people and "They shall see His face..." (Rev. 22:4). Thus, the New Testament ends with "Divine order restored to a disordered world," unified through the belief in one God. This is the Kingdom of God.

Unity is also furthered through ethical obedience—not simply lip service, but an allegiance of the heart (see Amos 5:21-24; Is. 29:13; Deut. 6:5; Prov. 4:23), whereby motive becomes as important as action. The Sermon on the Mount in Matthew's gospel taught that heart issues were an important root to the tree and fruit of our lives. Jesus maintained that obedience or disobedience to the law began inwardly in the human heart. It is not sufficient to conform one's outward actions and words to that which the law required.

The thought life must be conformed to the will of God
as expressed in the law first of all (see Ps. 40:8; Heb.
10:7,9). When the mind is set to do the will of God, the
speaking and acting will not deviate from it. Emphasis will be on the inward and spiritual aspects of
religion rather than on the outward and material
aspects.

Matthew 5 describes God's radical reconstruc-
tion of the heart. Observe the sequence. First,
we recognize we are in need (we're poor in spirit).
Next, *we repent of our self-sufficiency* (we
mourn). *We quit calling the shots and surrender
control to God* (we're meek). *So grateful are we
for His presence that we yearn for more of Him* (we
hunger and thirst). *As we grow closer to Him, we
become more like Him. We forgive others* (we're
merciful). *We change our outlook* (we're pure in
heart). *We love others* (we're peacemakers). *We endure injustice* (we're persecuted). *It's no casual
shift in attitude. It is a demolition of the old structure and a creation of the new. The more radical
the change, the greater the joy.*[16]

**Matthew 5 describes God's radical recon-
struction of the heart.**

1. **We recognize we are in need (we're poor
in spirit).**

2. **We repent of our self-sufficiency (we
mourn).**

---

16.   *The Applause of Heaven*, Max Lucado, p. 12, 1990, Word, Inc.
      Dallas, Texas. Used with permission.

3. We quit calling the shots and surrender control to God (we're meek).

4. So grateful are we for His presence that we yearn for more of Him (we hunger and thirst).

5. As we grow closer to Him, we become more like Him. We forgive others (we're merciful).

6. We change our outlook (we're pure in heart).

7. We love others (we're peacemakers).

8. We endure injustice (we're persecuted).

It's no casual shift in attitude. It is a demolition of the old structure and a creation of the new. The more radical the change, the greater the joy.

In accordance with God's will is His unchangeable character with certain moral attributes that belong to Him. These attributes are also those which God intends man to possess, and thus they are called communicable attributes. God is holy (see Lev. 11:45), and therefore so should we be holy. God is also perfect (see Mt. 5:48), truth (see Heb. 6:18), love (see 1 John 4:16), righteous (see Rom. 1:17), and faithful (see 1 Cor. 1:9). The moral character and qualities of God were manifested in Christ as the perfect man. These moral attributes are to be manifested in the believer also, as he is conformed to Christ. Only the Son of God, who was God incarnate, could give us a full and perfect revelation of the Father God. In Christ, God was clothed with the flesh of man. Jesus Christ was the fullest and clearest revelation of the Father and Son relationship that God desires the redeemed to come into by the new birth (see Jn. 1:14-18; 3:1-5; 14:9; 16:17; Mt. 5:45; 11:27; Ps. 103:13; 1 John 3:1-2).

These distinctive characteristics set apart the redeemed community from the unregenerate. The redeemed are bound together by their belief in one God and share the purpose of being light and salt to the world. The destiny of each individual and the entire called-out community is bound to a covenantal loyalty to one God, who both judges and blesses. God made man in His own image. His essential law for man is that he shall reflect the image of God and become like Him in character, demonstrating love that fulfills His covenants, faithfulness that discharges its responsibilities (see Lam. 3:23; Prov. 28:20), truthfulness that is reliable (see Ex. 34:6; Hos. 4:1), social concerns implemented in justice, with a balanced order that seeks compassionately to correct abuses (see Is. 30:18), righteousness that aims to conduct all its relationships with integrity and responsibility (Ps. 35:24; Deut. 6:25; Mk. 7:9).

Divine Enablement—Forgiveness

Every system of ethics must have some ultimate basis for goodness and obligation; God is the basis of Christian ethics. Buy why does God have authority over us? Why do we keep God's commandments? If we wish to respond by means of a coherent presentation of theology, there is more than one approach. One could start with human need. One could start by considering God's character, God's sovereignty, and God's intentions in creation and history and in the Law. But the question can be answered in terms of spiritual autobiography. The "why" now does not call for purely rational explanations, rather it asks why in fact you as a person seek to obey this God? It was with this question in mind that Karl Barth stated that God does not have authority over us because of a particular definition of God. We recognize this claim because God is "the God who is gracious to us in Christ Jesus." Barth here has encapsulated a central truth of New Testament theology and ethics. *Our obedience to God is inextricably bound up with our reception of divine grace in and following conversion.*[17]

... The law of the Spirit of life in Christ Jesus has made me free from the law of sin and death. For what the law could not do in that it was weak through the flesh, God did by sending His own Son in the likeness of sinful flesh, on account of sin: He condemned sin in the flesh [being sinless], *that the righteous requirement of the law might be fulfilled in us who do not walk according to the flesh but according to the Spirit* (Romans 8:2-4).

With the Christian answer it is now possible to understand that there are true moral absolutes. There is no law behind God, because the farthest

---

17.   Stephen C. Mott, *Biblical Ethics and Social Change* (New York: Oxford University Press, 1982), p. 23.

thing back is God. The moral absolutes rest upon God's character. The creation as He originally made it conformed to His character. The moral commands He has given to men are an expression of His character. Men as created in His image are to live by choice on the basis of what God is. *The standards of morality are determined by what conforms to His character, while those things which do not conform are immoral. ... When man sins, he brings forth what is contrary to the moral laws of the universe and as a result he is morally and legally guilty.*

The standards of morality are determined by what conforms to God's character, while those things which do not conform are immoral.

Because man is guilty before the Lawgiver of the universe, doing what is contrary to His character, his sin is significant in a significant history. Man has true moral guilt. This is entirely different from the conception of modern thought, which states that actions do not lead to guilt—a view within which actions thus become morally meaningless.[18]

To understand what the Apostle Paul means by the "law of sin and death," we must relate his understanding

18. Reprinted from *The God Who is There* by Francis A. Shaeffer. © 1968 by L 'Abri Fellowship, Switzerland. Used by permission of InterVarsity Press, P.O. Box 1400, Downers Grove, Illinois 60515.

of both sin and flesh. In reading Romans 8, we have little difficulty grasping the significance of the flesh. The law is said to be "weak through the flesh" (v. 3). Those who live "according to the flesh" set their minds on the "things of the flesh," which we are told is death (vv. 5-6). The fleshly mind is "enmity against God" and is not subject to the law of God, nor can it be (v. 7). "Those who are in the flesh cannot please God" (v. 8). The flesh is an attitude or inclination operating in complete rejection of the divine will, which requires self-sacrificial submission, choosing instead the free expression of anything and everything that will bring self-gratification. So pervasive is the sinful propensity of human nature, which seeks to be selfish and self-serving, that man recognizes he is incapable of breaking its power, resulting in his being "sold under sin."

The flesh is an attitude or inclination operating in complete rejection of the divine will, which requires self-sacrificial submission, choosing instead the free expression of anything and everything that will bring self-gratification.

God's grace is found in His dealings with the sinful human nature. God gave the law which could neither make man right with God nor make him live rightly before God. God sent "His own Son in the likeness of sinful flesh, and for sin..." (Rom. 8:3, KJV). He knew no sin (see 2 Cor. 5:21). Christ came for sin as a sin offering. He condemned sin by assuming our sin on the cross. Sentence was passed and executed on sin in Christ's flesh. Those who are "in Christ" have identified

with Him in His condemnation of sin in the flesh and
in so doing have taken the first step to living free of
its dominion.

God's redeeming grace has two aspects. One,
grace is God's power for us, the works of pardon
and justification through atonement by the Son.
Second, grace is also God's power in us, the work
of sanctification by the Spirit of God, as well as
the Spirit's work in drawing us to repentance
and transforming us. As God's power in us, *grace
gives us strength to be what we cannot be in ourselves.* The Spirit empowers us to act ethically,
including social action, as grace "reigns through
righteousness for eternal life" (Rom. 5:21).

God's redeeming grace has two aspects.

**1. Grace is God's power for us, the works of
   pardon and justification through atonement by the Son.**

**2. Grace is also God's power in us, the work
   of sanctification by the Spirit of God, as
   well as the Spirit's work in drawing us to
   repentance and transforming us.**

The obedience invoked by what God is and does
is dependent upon our wills alone, for God works
in us through both our will and our actions for
God's own purpose (Phil. 2:11-12).[19]

Christian holiness is not a matter of painstaking
conformity to the specific precepts of an external law

---

19.   Mott, op. cit. p. 27.

code; it is rather a question of the Holy Spirit producing His fruit in our life, reproducing those graces which were seen in perfection in the life of Christ. All that the law required by way of conforming to the will of God is now realized in the lives of those who are controlled by the Holy Spirit and are released from their servitude to the old order. *God's commands have now become God's enablings.*

Divine Sanction—Holiness

To fully understand holiness we need to realize that it involves "two sides to the same coin." On one side is God's part in the sanctifying, consecrating process, and on the other hand, man has his important part. God makes us holy (sanctifies us, separates us) (Jn. 17:16-17; Heb. 2:11; Eph. 5:25-27; 2 Thess. 2:13b). Man must sanctify himself (set apart, separate) (2 Cor. 7:1; 2 Tim. 2:21; 1 Sam. 16:5; Lev. 11:44; 20:7-8). Isaiah 6:3-7 shows us that God alone is absolute holiness, He only is purely holy. Man is not holy, inherently. Yet God chooses. God calls. God commissions. Holiness is a gift, an unearned grace-gift from God. God's holiness becomes reality in the people of God (1 Pet. 2:9) by positioning us in Christ. But we can frustrate this gift by corrupting, compromising and conceding to worldly conduct, cultural philosophies, etc. Therefore His endowed people, His "holy ones" are not to turn from the life of holiness, but are to continually purge themselves, to "perfect holiness." God has "separated" us by His calling; we must respond

by "separating" ourselves from worldly influence. That is our holy calling. That is what
holiness is all about.[20]

God wants to give us power for worthy living (see
1 Thes. 4:7). Jesus' purpose in the incarnation is to
"save His people from their sins" (Mt. 1:21). His
atonement had in view man's redemption "from every
lawless deed and [to] purify for Himself His own special people, zealous for good works" (Tit. 2:14). Its end
is not simply deliverance from hell and its misery. It
is a rescue and recovery mission by which there is an
impartation of a holy principle into our lives: restoration of the divine image of purity, reestablishment of
communion with the Holy God, ethical recovery and
restoration whereby men cease to be and do evil and
learn to be and do good. The life of the Spirit of Christ
in the individual believer is the very life of Christ in
him reproducing the character of Christ by "forming
Christ" within his heart. The holiness of the believer
results in fruitfulness, (see Mk. 4:26-29).

**The life of the Spirit of Christ in the in-
dividual believer is the very life of Christ in
him reproducing the character of Christ by
"forming Christ" within his heart.**

The nature of the fruit depends on the nature of
the parent plant. The spirit-filled life leads to the life
of Christlike conduct. Christ can and does actually

---

20.   Dick Iverson, *Holiness: The Unique Escape from Oblivion* (New
       York: Ministers Fellowship International, 1992), p. 5-6.

give Himself to, share His mind with, put His Spirit
into those who really seek the will of God for their
lives.

> **The spirit-filled life leads to the life of
> Christlike conduct. Christ can and does ac-
> tually give Himself to, share His mind with,
> put His Spirit into those who really seek the
> will of God for their lives.**

In order to know the will of God we must have a
clear understanding of how God's law relates to us in
and through Christ. To make a law legitimate it must
be sanctioned. Sanction can be defined as "the
authoritative approval or permission making a course
of action valid" and also "a consideration, influence, or
principle dictating ethical choice." It can be further
defined as "a law or decree; the penalty for noncom-
pliance specified in a law or decree; a penalty,
specified or in the form of moral pressure, that acts to
ensure compliance or conformity."[21]

> The significance of the Law is that it inscrip-
> turates God's command in propositional form as
> a fixed rule of life. As such, it is an expression of
> God's eternal moral will, grounded ultimately in
> the very being of God. The Law tells what the
> eternally righteous Creator and Lord requires of
> His creatures. Since it is based on the nature
> and purpose of the changeless God, the Law can

---

21.   *Webster's II New Riverside University Dictionary,* op. cit.
      p. 1035.

never be abolished, but remains forever. Not even Christ abrogates the Law taken in this sense, nor is the divine salvation of sinners by grace accomplished in violation of the moral law or in disregard to justice. ...The law in its Mosaic form of administration is fulfilled by Jesus Christ. The Christian is "not under law" (Rom. 6:14; Gal. 5:18), he is "dead to law" (Rom. 7:4, Gal. 2:19), he is "redeemed from under law" (Gal. 4:5). The law as part of the Mosaic economy, whether ceremonial or moral, has no claim against the believer. Its requirements are met for him, and his salvation is secured for him by the merits of Jesus Christ. ...The law itself looks ahead to the moral law inscribed upon the hearts of men by the Spirit of God (Jer. 31:33). The law of Moses was not given as the way of salvation by works; it presupposed the Abrahamic covenant of grace, and it was addressed to the children of promise, to the chosen people. ...The eternal moral law of God is binding on the believer and unbeliever alike.

The law of Moses was not given as the way of salvation by works; it presupposed the Abrahamic covenant of grace, and it was addressed to the children of promise, to the chosen people.

To the believer, this is not a predicament of terror for the sole reason that the Savior has met the full demand of the law and is the ground of his salvation. But believer and unbeliever alike are answerable to the divine moral demand. God condemns one because the law's demands are not met by him; He spares the other because they are met in a substitute.[22]

Believer and unbeliever alike are answerable to the divine moral demand. God condemns one because the law's demands are not met by him; He spares the other because they are met in a substitute.

God's will expressed through the law can be under stood in a threefold purpose: political, spiritual, and moral. In the first use...

...the law functions to restrain sin and maintain order in the world. God has ordained earthly government for this purpose (Mt. 22:17-21; Rom. 13:1-7; 1 Tim. 2:1-4; Titus 3:1-11; 1 Pet. 2:13-17). The second use of the law is the proclamation of God's wrath against sin. In this use, the accusing voice of the law works within the sinner to reveal sin and destroy self-righteous pride (Rom. 3:19,20; 7:7; Gal. 2:19). The ultimate purpose is to bring the sinner to see his need for Christ and to be saved (Gal. 3:23,24; 1 Tim. 2:1-4). The third use of the law applies only to Christians. It is the call to Christians to "put off" the old nature and flee from sin. This use is necessary because Christians are still sinners who are continually tempted to return to the flesh (namely, the rule of self). But this use of the law is only possible because they are reborn with a new nature

22.   Henry, op. cit. p. 350-353

that delights in the law and desires to be rid of the flesh (Rom. 7:22-25; Col. 3:5-10). This third use is the exhortation to continue in grace, to resist the flesh, and to yield to the Spirit (Rom. 6:12-14; 8:12-14). Inevitably, this exhortation includes moral guidance (Rom. 12:14–13:14; Gal. 5:16–6:2; Eph. 4:25–6:9; Col. 3:5–4:6; 1 Thess. 4:1-8). It also includes the warning that those who return to the flesh, whether in legalistic or lawless ways, "will not inherit the Kingdom of God" (1 Cor. 6:9-10; Gal. 3:1-10; 5:19-21; Eph. 5:5). The moral law is thus valid for the Christian, not as a means of salvation, but as a guide in sanctification.[23]

The moral law is thus valid for the Christian, not as a means of salvation, but as a guide in sanctification.

Thus we conclude that the law was never designed to offer anyone eternal life; it has never been intended to be set in opposition to the promises of God. ...The moral law, as revealed in the Old Testament, was the recognized standard of holiness that remained authoritative for Christ, the apostles, and the early church because it was written. It is proper to speak of the law as being "done away with" or of our having been "set free from" it only in the sense that now in Christ has the law reached its proper end and goal, for He perfectly fulfilled its commands in His life as well as His death.

23. R.K. Harrison, ed., *Encyclopedia of Biblical and Christian Ethics* (Nashville, Tennessee: Thomas Nelson Publishers, 1987), p. 226.

Thus we conclude that the law was never designed to offer anyone eternal life; it has never been intended to be set in opposition to the promises of God. The moral law, as revealed in the Old Testament, was the recognized standard of holiness that remained authoritative for Christ, the apostles, and the early church because it was written.

Thus, we believers are finished with the law in its ceremonial demands and ceremonial sanctions, but we will continue to find an abiding use for the law in these areas: The moral law continues to function as one of Scripture's formal teachers on what is right and wrong in conduct. The moral law continues to provide standards by which men and women are convinced and convicted of their sin and guilt. We had not known sin, in some cases, except God's law had shown it for what it was. The moral law is a coercive force helping the redeemed to spot moral imperfections that still cling to their lives as they "are being changed from glory to glory."[24]

In following the moral law of God, we have to guard ourselves from a legalistic attitude. A legalist could be described as...

...one who adheres rigidly to moral rules and does not exercise sufficient flexibility in the application

24. Taken from the book, TOWARD OLD TESTAMENT ETHICS by Walter C. Kaiser, Jr. pp. 308-312. Copyright © 1983 by Zondervan Publishing House. Used by permission of Zondervan Publishing House.

of those rules to the human situation. ...Often accompanying the use of the term *legalist* is the implicit suggestion that the offending party is not sufficiently motivated by compassion or human concern.[25]

A legalist could be described as one who adheres rigidly to moral rules and does not exercise sufficient flexibility in the application of those rules to the human situation.

The religious party of the Pharisees, during the time of Jesus, offers a case study in moralistic thinking. Ironically most of the opposition Jesus faced was not pagan but religious. ...The Pharisees advocated a precise and carefully nuanced interpretation of biblical law. Their aim was to apply the law in every conceivable situation. In time, they added to the biblical commands a tradition of by-laws and applications designed to ensure an exacting program of Righteousness. ...It is not difficult to understand why attention shifted from the fundamental concerns of justice, mercy, and faithfulness to the specific details of dietary laws, tithing codes, and Sabbath rules. Obedience was reduced to a measurable performance test. Their zeal for the finer points of the law resulted in the formation of small communities dedicated to preserving their ceremonial purity and tithing obligations. Jesus was a threat to this approach to ethics. He was concerned with divorce, lust, anger, power,

---

25.   Harrison, op. cit. p. 229.

wealth, revenge, and lying. The Pharisees were
concerned with tithing their spices, keeping up
their image, and preserving their national identity. Jesus explored the heart; the Pharisees
judged on appearance.[26]

A clearer understanding of how we are to follow
the law of God and not enter into legalism would
come as a result of understanding the difference
between laws, principles, and rules. From the
transcultural, unalterable, universal laws which
God has given, we develop principles. Principles are guidelines for action based on a synthesis of the collected body of information or
teaching related to a specific law. Principles
are drawn from three or four passages of God's
Word because God's Word does not always have
a specific law laid out for every action. Six
hundred and thirteen laws were given to the
Jewish people. These were later reduced in essence to three: Love, justice and to show mercy.
Christ ultimately brought them down to one:
"You shall love the Lord your God with all your
heart and your neighbor as yourself." This became the law. Paul said: "By love serve one
another." In essence, the whole law can be
reduced to one word: love. From the law, the law
of love, we get principles for living. From principles we develop rules.

---

26. Taken from the book, CHOICES OF THE HEART by
     Douglas D. Webster, pp. 41-42. Copyright © 1990 by Douglas
     Webster. Used by permission of Zondervan Publishing House.

Principles are guidelines for action based on a synthesis of the collected body of information or teaching related to a specific law.

Rules are guidelines for individual or corporate arrangements to assist individuals in fulfilling principles or laws. Rules may be culturally oriented.

Rules are guidelines for individual or corporate arrangements to assist individuals in fulfilling principles or laws.

Rules are usually based on an effort to fulfill the Spirit of the principle or the law.[27]

Our confusion comes when we elevate our rules to an equal value with the laws that God has revealed. We cannot possibly interpret God's law apart from God's Spirit. God's law expresses to us His love. It provides for us a pathway to freedom and wholeness. The commandments were not given to limit our freedom or focus on punishment. They were given to point the pathway to purposeful living and fulfillment. The same God who spoke the Commandments spoke through Jesus when He said, "I have come that they may have life, and that they may have it more abundantly" (Jn. 10:10).

---

27.   James D. Cunningham and Anthony C. Fortosis, *Education in Christian Schools: A Perspective and Training Model* (Whittier, California: The Association of Christian Schools International, 1987), pp. 104-105.

The Commandments are laws of love and relationships that lead us to responsible behavior. The principles of these laws lead us to a loving relationship with God and with each other. We receive the affirmation and acceptance of being children of God. Through these principles we have direction for making right choices, for it is the choices we make in life that affect our happiness or unhappiness, not only in this world, but the world to come.

Clearer understanding of what God is like is learned through His commandments. They teach us what it means to be human. Only humans can disobey God. Also, only humans can willingly choose to obey God. Within the realm of our possibilities are both obedience and disobedience. Our choice, a result of our inner thinking, finds its outward expression in what we say and in our actions (see Prov. 23:7; Jn. 7:38).

The Ten Commandments pertain to the very foundations of our personal lives. We are free to choose. The exercise of that freedom, however, does have consequences. We are free to say "yes" or "no" to God, but our lives reveal the consequences of those choices. No one really "breaks" the commandments. If we are disobedient, they break us. We live in a universe governed by laws. If we step off a roof, we fall victim to the law of gravity. Moral and spiritual laws also must be followed, or we fall victim to their consequences. For every action there is a reaction. God has given guides so that we may find freedom, love, meaning, and purpose. God's commandments are meant to be a light for our journey. Psalm 119:105 states, "Your Word is a lamp to my feet and a light for my path."

> God's commandment, revealed in Jesus Christ, embraces the whole of life. It does not only, like the ethical, keep watch on the untransgressible frontier of life, but it is at the same time the center and the fulness of life. ...It becomes the element in which one lives without always being conscious of it, and, thus it implies freedom of movement or of action, freedom from the fear of decision, freedom from fear to act, it implies certainty, quietude, confidence, balance and peace.[28]

Part of the majesty and mystery of our humanity is that God created us capable of choice, and He wants us to choose life by choosing Him, His way, and His will. But the choice is always ours.

Divine Mission—Witness

Jesus, before ascending into Heaven, left His followers with a vision and a command to carry out. "Go into all the world," He charged them, "and preach the gospel to every creature" (Mk. 16:15). They would have the promise of the Father—the Holy Spirit—to enable them to complete this divine mission, that the words spoken by the prophet Isaiah might be fulfilled: "...all the ends of the earth shall see the salvation of our God" (Is. 52:10). The challenge for these men, as Jesus poured out His Spirit and gave birth to the

---

28.   Bonhoeffer, op. cit. p. 280.

Jerusalem church, was to structure this body of believers in such a way as to be able to fulfill this mandate. A proper structuring of the church was needed in order for the gospel to be carried to a lost world. It had to be based upon a divine pattern and blueprint.

This divine pattern is something that is revealed through the Word of God, by the Spirit of God, in the timing of God. God spoke to Ezekiel to make known to the people of Israel the "law of the temple" (see Ezek. 43:10-12), to instruct them in its design, its arrangement, its exits and entrances, all its laws. He further instructed him to write it down so that they could keep its whole design, its ordinances, and perform them.

The Lord also spoke to Habbakuk, the prophet, and instructed him to "Write the vision and make it plain on tablets, that he may run who reads it. For the vision is yet for an appointed time; but at the end it will speak, and it will not lie. Though it tarries, wait for it; because it will surely come, it will not tarry" (Hab. 2:2-3).

The Book of Proverbs tells us something about vision, or in some cases the lack of it. "Where there is no vision, the people are unrestrained..." (Prov. 29:18, NAS). Unrestrained people are like a stampede of wild horses running in all directions, each one having different ideas about what to do and how to do it. One pulls toward his favorite idea, and another pulls in the opposite direction. Too many visions having little relationship with God's overall vision cause the Church to lose direction and destiny.

We find that the Old Testament temple was a type of the New Testament Church, a called-out community of God's people, who are being built on a foundation which included the apostles and prophets with Jesus Christ, Himself, being the Chief Cornerstone. In Him the whole building is joined together to grow into a holy temple in the Lord for a habitation of God in the Spirit.

God's vision is plain: Christ is the builder, working in His people by the indwelling of the Holy Spirit to build His Church, to accomplish His Father's vision and bring glory to Him. The Church was not to be a mere religious organization based upon outward conformances, but a corporate expression of Christ's life working within His many membered body.

God's threefold vision then is that we be individually and personally conformed to Jesus Christ, knowing Him and being like Him in all things; that all believers in Christ be in complete unity in the bonds of covenant love; and that the gospel be preached to all men in every nation on earth.

God's vision is threefold:

  1. That we be individually and personally conformed to Jesus Christ, knowing Him and being like Him in all things.

  2. That all believers in Christ be in complete unity in the bonds of covenant love.

3. That the gospel be preached to all men in every nation on earth.

God's vision gave birth to His mission that was to have a people become a witness to His rule. God's will was to bring unity to all of life. He revealed Himself through the law and the prophets and more fully through His Son, Jesus. Through the sinless life of Christ and His death, burial, and resurrection we can have forgiveness of sins and the enabling power of the Holy Spirit to walk holy before Him. Now He calls us not only individually but corporately, to become a community which is visible rather than obscure. We are called to accomplish a task—discipleship with a purpose.

Jesus revealed the nature of the witness we are to have as His disciples in this world in His discourse, the Sermon on the Mount. As witnesses there must be a revelation to the world. We must be seen. We are the light of the world (Mt. 5:14). Light must shine. It's the nature of light to be seen. Light is a positive, aggressive force combatting darkness. It's a force of justice and triumph. Light is a service for those who, having eyes to see, need the path to their destiny illuminated.

Light is also a symbol of salvation and life. Believers are the only ones who can show the world the way to salvation. They are called to demonstrate what God can do in a transformed life. To remain invisible would be a denial of the call of God. A community that hides has ceased to follow the Lord. Jesus hammered home this point by likening this community to "a city set on a hill." A city is made up of people functioning under a government, with a particular identity that distinguishes it from other cities. God's people are to be an example of a body wherein the rule of God is present and His light seen.

Jesus also likened His people to salt. Salt is both a preserver and a flavoring agent. It is a most indispensable necessity of life. It symbolized the strength and truthfulness of the people's self-surrender as they declared their loyalty, dependence on God, and willingness to serve Him (see Lev. 2:13). The disciples of the Lord are a supreme value to the world, without which it could not live. Their lives are to be a sustaining power on the earth. Only as salt retains its cleansing and flavoring properties can salt preserve the earth. Salt must remain salt. We must remain faithful to the mission to which Christ has called us. But how is this body made visible?

Let's look at the commissioning process given in Matthew 28:19-20. First we are told to make disciples, then baptize them in Christ, and finally to teach them to observe all commands. This reveals the responsibility of the discipling Church as it goes out to fulfill the commission of the Lord. First, we must make the lost into disciples of or learners of Christ, then we bring them to a decision to be identified with Christ and immersed into Christ. Finally we give them instruction in the commandments of the Lord, including how to relate to the new community of believers.

This divine pattern can be seen in the Book of Acts 2:38-41. Peter preached the first message of the early Church following Pentecost, when those gathered in the upper room were filled with the Holy Spirit. The outcome was that those who received His word were baptized and were added. To what were they added? They were added to the Church (see Acts 2:47). Note what followed as the Church continued in the apostles' teachings.

The apostles were men chosen by God to bear witness to the events of His revelation in Jesus Christ. They were eyewitnesses (see 1 John 1:1-4), foundation builders (Eph. 2:20), carrying the Word of God, not the word of men (1 Thess. 2:13). The sum of the apostles' teaching was "Christ in His Church."

In the life of the Church, one cannot separate the individual disciple from the Body of Jesus. In the Christian life they belong inseparably together (see Acts 2:42). The infant Church of Acts 2 was a visible community which all the world could see. They had "favor with all the people" (Acts 2:47). The Lord added to them day by day those that would be saved. The daily growth of the Church is the proof of the power of the Lord who dwells in it.

Everything the disciple does either is or should be part of the common life of the church of which he is a member. There is no department of life in which the members may withdraw from the Body, nor should we desire to withdraw. It is our baptism into the Body of Christ which assures us of a full share in the life of Christ and the Church. When a man is baptized into the Body of Christ, not only is his personal status in regard to salvation changed, but also the relationship of daily life. In baptism, we are grafted into the vine of the Lord. This involves a cutting away of our former position and a grafting into a new state. The seal of this baptism is the Holy Spirit, who confirms that the transplanted branch has taken hold of its new position in Christ. It is through this new relationship that the believer will grow and prosper in the fruit of God's Spirit. Whatever we are, whatever we do, everything happens in the Body, in the Church, in Christ. This is how the Church invades the life of the world and conquers territory for Christ. The member in the Body of Christ has been delivered from the world and called out of it; He must give the world a visible proof of his calling.

If we are to be both salt and light, then we must exhibit the purity of the Lord's holiness, while at the same time being an example of God's love. The early Church continued in the apostles' doctrine and had all things in common.

If we are to be both salt and light, then we must exhibit the purity of the Lord's holiness, while at the same time being an example of God's love.

Note that the commandments given to the apostles were meant to be taught to a body of believers. The purity that needed to be exhibited by Christ's followers was not something that they could manufacture nor complete through observance. Only through baptism into the Body of Christ and the baptism of the Holy Spirit could the believer have the power necessary to overcome sin in his life. The body of believers were to encourage each other in covenant love to the holiness of God.

There is a need for the simultaneous practice of two biblical principles. The first is the principle of the practice of purity of the visible church. The scriptures teach that we must practice, not just talk about, the purity of the visible church. The second is the principle of an observable love and oneness among all true Christians. The mark of a Christian stresses from John 13:34,35 that according to Jesus Himself, the world has the right to decide whether we are true Christians, true disciples of Christ on the basis of the love we show to all true Christians. John 17:21 provides something even more sobering in that Jesus gives the world the right to judge whether the Father has sent the Son on the basis of whether the world sees observable love among all true Christians.

One cannot explain the explosive dynamite, the *dunamis,* of the early church apart from the fact that they practiced two things simultaneously: orthodoxy of doctrine and orthodoxy of community in the midst of the visible church, a community which the world could see. By the grace of God, therefore, the church must be known simultaneously for its purity of doctrine and the reality of its community.

> **By the grace of God, therefore, the church must be known simultaneously for its purity of doctrine and the reality of its community.**

We have, then, two sets of parallel couplets: (1) the principle of the practice of the purity of the visible church, and yet the practice of observable love among all true Christians; and (2) the practice of orthodoxy of doctrine and observable orthodoxy of community in the visible church.

The heart of these sets of principles is to show forth the love of God and the holiness of God simultaneously. If we show either of these without the other, we exhibit not the character, but a caricature of God for the world to see. If we stress the love of God without the holiness of God, it turns out to be a compromise. But if we stress the holiness of God without the love of God, we practice something that is hard and lacks beauty. ...In the name of our Lord Jesus Christ, we are called upon to show a watching world and to our young people that the church is something beautiful![29]

The human body is God's masterpiece in creation (Gen. 1:26-28; 2:7; Ps. 139:13-17). With its untold millions (perhaps 30-50 million) of cells,

---

29. From *The Church Before the Watching World* by Francis A Shaeffer. © 1971 by InterVarsity Press. All rights reserved. Reprinted in 1991 by Crossway Books as Vol. 4 of *The Complete Works of Francis A. Schaeffer—A Christian Worldview*. p. 152.

etc., its marvelous nervous system of communication, the blood, the skin, the arms and legs and feet, the heart, liver, kidneys, lungs, brains, head, eyes, ears, the protective structure of the bones (at least 246 bones in the body, 63 in the head, 24 in the sides, 16 in the wrist, 14 in the joints, 108 in the hands and feet), etc., and the wonder of all these working together in marvelous harmony and unity in the one body of man—all is indeed the marvel of the divine creation.

If God did this in the old creation man, what shall He do in the new creation man—the body of Christ? He desires to relive His life in the Church which is His body. There are millions of unseen members in the natural body, as well as the seen. Yet all work together in harmony for a whole and healthy body. The unseen and visible members and cells maintain the seen and visible in active health and life. There are no "independent" members in the body. Every joint supplies (see Eph. 4:16)."[30]

Because of the unique purpose which God has made known, because of the tremendous plan God has for the Body and because of the intricate interrelationships in the Body, no true believer can find fulfillment and accomplishment outside the Body of Christ, the Church. Just as Christ's natural body was visible, even

---

30. Kevin J. Conner, *The Church in the New Testament* (Portland, Oregon: Bible Temple Publishing, 1989), p. 78.

so His present Body has its visible expression. To fail to identify with the visible Body of Christ or the local Church is to sever yourself from the Body. As soon as you cut off your foot, that foot loses its function.

To fail to identify with the visible body of Christ or the local church is to sever yourself from the body.

The foot only has a function as it relates to the body. Our ministries are only useful or edifying to the Body as they are properly related to the Body. When they are properly related, the life-giving blood will flow to cleanse, heal and nourish each and every member of the Body.

There is something even more severe if we cut ourselves off from the Church, the Body of Christ. When a person rejects the Body, he rejects the Head. A severed foot no longer responds to the commands and directions of the brain. When a person rejects the Body, he rejects God's chain of command and becomes a law unto himself. This is lawlessness. God calls it rebellion.

When a person rejects the body, he rejects God's chain of command and becomes a law unto himself. This is lawlessness. God calls it rebellion.

There are many today who desire to be used of God, but they refuse to come under the authority of the Body of Christ. When we understand what the Body means to God, it is not hard for us to see why rebellion is condemned so harshly by Him (Is. 1:19-23; 1 Sam. 15:23; Prov. 17:11; Jer. 28:16; Ps. 68:6; Mt. 7:21-23).

God gives us strict instructions not to forsake the assembling of ourselves together. As we gather as the Body of Christ, we will be strengthened, the Body will be built up and the purpose of God will be accomplished in and through Christ's Body, the Church.[31]

We must maintain a balanced view of the Church's purpose.

For the church to have a corrective impact on the culture it must maintain a separate and distinct identity from the surrounding society and any new society that it may help to create. Mission is consistent with separation as long as it is kept in mind that the motivation for that separation is mission, and not separation for its own sake. The only way to really retain true spiritual values is to quicken them with the divine imperative of witnessing to the world. This dynamic nonconformity finds its base in scripture (rather than in the culture of two generations ago) and those who live by it will be enabled to give moral and spiritual direction to the world.[32]

---

31.   Dick Iverson, *Present Day Truths* (Portland, Oregon: Bible Temple Publishing, 1975), pp. 164-165.
32.   Mott, op. cit. p. 133.

Divine Preparation—Faithfulness (Bride)

The revelation given to Paul concerning the Church as the great mystery, the Bride of Christ, shows the ultimate intention of the Lord for His Church (Eph. 5:23-32). This is Godward in its truth even as the earlier revelations were outward and inward in their truths.

The Church is to be: *A sanctified Church that is holy, separated unto the Lord; a cleansed Church, by the washing of water by the Word; a glorious Church, clothed with glory and bringing glory to Christ; a Church without spot or wrinkle, even as the Old Testament sacrifices were to be without spot, wrinkle, blemish or any such thing; a holy Church, separated from sin; a Church like unto Christ so that He can be united to her and not have an unequal yoke in this marriage.*

The word has gone forth out of the mouth of the Lord and the zeal of the Lord of Hosts will perform it (Is. 55:9-11). This is the kind of Church He will have.[33]

Throughout Scripture there is a special relationship between God and His people. God likens this relationship to a marriage in which He is the husband and Israel His wife (see Jer. 3:14).

Throughout Scripture there is a special relationship between God and His people.

---

33.   Conner, p. 29.

The great mystery of which Paul speaks is Christ becoming the divine Bridegroom and the Church His Bride.

When you examine the New Testament, you find that the brideship is thought of in two ways. In some places the emphasis is upon the fact that each Christian is, individually, the Bride of Christ, and in other places it is the church as a unity that is the Bride of Christ. But there is no contradiction in this; there is merely unity in the midst of diversity. The church is collectively the Bride of Christ, and it is made up of individual Christians, each one of whom is the Bride of Christ.[34] John the Baptist testified of Jesus as the Bridegroom (see Jn. 3:28-29). The relationship of Christ and His Church (His people) is described in terms of the covenant of marriage with Christ being the husband and the Church, His wife.

Furthermore, the apostle Paul describes the relationship of the believer to Christ in these terms: "Therefore, my brethren, you also have become dead to the law through the body of Christ, that you may be married to another, even to Him who was raised from the dead, that we should bear fruit to God" (Rom. 7:4).

In order to understand the relationship we have by being married to Christ, we must compare the

---

34. Schaeffer, *A Christian View of the Church*, op. cit. Vol. 4. p. 134.

relationship God's people had with the law in terms of a marriage relationship.

Those people who see their hope of being justified centered in their relationship to the law do
not have happy marriages to the law. Married as
they are to the law which is perfect, inflexible,
demanding, and all-encompassing, they are
soon driven to despair by their own incapability,
in the same way that tender young brides have
been known to be destroyed by domineering husbands whose rectitude was matched only by
their insensitivity. Paul outlined something of
the pressures experienced by the brides of the
law when he wrote, "Cursed is every one that
continueth not in all things which are written in
the book of the law to do them" (Gal. 3:10).

If we may take the marriage analogy a little further, we can imagine what it must be like for a
bride to be confronted each day by a husband
who has a list of things which must be done
thoroughly and perfectly. She must continue to
do them; she must not only think about them
but actually perform them. No half measures
will be tolerated; no concessions to weakness
will be made. There will be no excuses, no explanations will be asked for or given, and every
failure in every case will result in the unfor-
tunate bride being cursed for her ineptitude
and incompetence. To add insult to injury, the
enraged husband will then proceed to live in
total inflexible adherence to his own impossible

demands, humiliating the bride even more.
...His exemplary behavior is a witness to the
perfection of his own demands but also the im-
perfection of her abilities. The resultant breakdown of relationship reaches culmination when,
upon the death of Mr. Law, the bride breathes
more sighs of relief than she sheds tears of
remorse. No longer must she embark each morn-
ing on an impossible task, knowing full well that
she must face each evening in the inevitable condemnation of Mr. Perfection. She is free![35]

Max Lucado describes...

...a story of a woman who for years was married
to a harsh husband. Each day he would leave
her a list of chores to complete before he returned
at the end of the day. "Clean the yard. Stack the
firewood. Wash the windows... ." If she didn't
complete the tasks, she would be greeted with
his explosive anger. But even if she did complete
the list, he was never satisfied; he would always
find inadequacies in her work. After several
years, the husband passed away. Some time
later she remarried, this time to a man who
lavished her with tenderness and adoration.
One day, while going through a box of old papers,
the wife discovered one of her first husband's
lists. And as she read the sheet, a realization

35. *The Communicator's Commentary: Vol. 6, Romans,* D. Stuard
    Briscoe, pp. 142-143, 1982, Word, Inc., Dallas, Texas. Used
    with permission.

caused a tear of joy to splash on the paper. "I'm still doing all these things, and no one has to tell me. I do it because I love him."[36]

"Life under the law is a never-ending list of rules and regulations which produce a never-ending stream of fears and frustrations. But marriage to Christ is a relationship of love which freely submits and obeys with delight."[37]

> Having been raised from the dead, He will die no more (Rom. 6:9); therefore this new marriage relationship will not be broken by death, as the old one was. ...The fruit of the marriage is a new life, characterized by good works, which God prepared beforehand, that we should walk in them (Eph. 2:10).[38]

Life under the law is a never-ending list of rules and regulations which produce a never-ending stream of fears and frustrations. But marriage to Christ is a relationship of love which freely submits and obeys with delight.

These works are not the means to justification, but simply the response of a bride displaying her love for her bridegroom resulting in fruitfulness.

---

36. Lucado, op. cit. p. 176.
37. Briscoe, op. cit. p. 144.
38. F.F. Bruce, *Tyndale New Testament Commentaries: Romans* (Grand Rapids, Michigan: William B. Eerdmans Publishing Company, reprinted 1988), p. 138.

The love of Christ for His church revealed in this figure (bride) is an outstanding demonstration of the love of God. Five characteristics of divine love may be mentioned. (1) The eternal duration of the love of God stems from the fact that "God is love" (1 John 4:8). (2) The love of God is the motivation for His ceaseless activity. (3) The love of God has transparent purity. (4) The love of God has limitless intensity (Rom. 8:39). (5) The love of God has inexhaustible benevolence.[39]

God's love can be understood further as we continue in this analogy of marriage. Think of all the preparations that a bride makes in order to present herself to her husband in all her beauty.

She wants to be seen lovely and in splendor, without spot or wrinkle or any such thing. So the church is to appear before her heavenly bridegroom (Rev. 21:2). But the difference in this case is that she can do nothing of herself to make herself beautiful in the eyes of her Lord. Of necessity it is all His work. He must thus present the church to Himself. The word translated *in splendor (endoxon)* speaks of honor, of glory, of beauty, but it is implied that the church owes "all her glory to His work." She can only be *without spot or wrinkle,* the stains of

---

39. Taken from the book, MAJOR BIBLE THEMES by Lewis Sperry Chafter and John F. Walvoord, pp. 279-280. Copyright © 1974 by Dallas Theological Seminary. Used by permission of Zondervan Publishing House.

sin, and the decadence of age, through what is
effected by His sanctifying and renewing work.[40]

In this relationship the bride needs to be found
faithful. Anything that is apart from faith is sin. The
bride is called to be a virgin and given only to one.
Throughout Scripture there are contrasting themes of
the true and the apostate; the pure virgin and the
harlot woman. In contrast with Israel, who is the unfaithful wife of Jehovah, the Church is pictured in the
New Testament as the virgin bride awaiting the com-
ing of her Bridegroom (see 2 Cor. 11:2). The uniting of
man and woman in marriage is a picture of the intentions of God in the relationship of Christ and the
Church.

> Marriage among the Jews of Paul's day involved
> two separate ceremonies, the betrothal and the
> nuptial ceremony which consummated the mar-
> riage. Usually a year elapsed between the two,
> but during that period the girl was regarded
> legally as the man's wife, while socially she
> remained a virgin. The betrothal contract was
> binding, and could be broken only by death or a
> formal written divorce. Unfaithfulness or viola-
> tion of a betrothed girl was regarded as adultery
> and punishable as such. ...Paul sees himself as
> the agent of God through whom his converts
> were betrothed to Christ, and feels under obliga-
> tion to ensure that they are presented as a pure

40. Francis Foulkes, *Tyndale New Testament Commentaries:
     Ephesians* (Grand Rapids, Michigan: William B. Eerdmans
     Publishing Company, 1989), p. 166.

virgin to her one husband at the nuptial ceremony when the marriage will be consummated (2 Cor. 11:2-3).[41]

"There is a place for a spiritual father's passionate concern for the exclusive and pure devotion to Christ of his spiritual children, and also a place for anger at potential violators of the purity (2 Cor. 11:29)."[42] Paul was warning the Corinthian church that they needed to produce fruit likened to the bridegroom or else they were being unfaithful. What is wrong when the right kind of fruit is not being grown (see Rom. 7:4)? The branch must be abiding in the wrong tree (see Rom. 6:13-21).

There are reasons why we may not be bringing forth the fruit we should. It may be because of ignorance, because we may never have been taught the meaning of the work of Christ for our present lives. There are five possible "ignorances" in this area. First, the Christian may have been taught how to be justified, but never taught the present meaning of the work of Christ for him. Second, he may have been taught to become a Christian through the instrumentality of faith, but then he may have been left, as though from that point on the

41. Colin Kruse, *Tyndale New Testament Commentaries: 2 Corinthians* (Grand Rapids, Michigan: William B. Eerdmans Publishing Company, 1989), p. 183.
42. Ralph W. Harris, ed., The New Testament Study Bible: Romans Corinthians (Missouri: The Complete Bible Library, 1989), Vol. 7, p. 611.

Christian life has to be lived in his own strength. Third, he may have been taught the opposite. That is, that having accepted Christ, in some antinomian way it does not now matter how he lives. Fourth, he may have been taught some kind of second blessing, which would make him perfect in this life when he receives it. This the Bible does not teach. And therefore he just waits hopelessly, or tries to act upon that which does not exist. Fifth, he may never have been taught that there is a reality of faith to be acted on consciously after justification. This last point is the point of ignorance of many who stand in the orthodox and historic stream of the Reformation.

Because of any of these ignorances, the Christian may not "possess his possessions" in this present life. But when a man does learn the meaning of the work of Christ in the present life, a new door is open to him. And this new door then seems to be so wonderful that often it gives the Christian, as he begins to act upon the knowledge of faith, the sense of something that is as new as was his conversion.[43]

As we continue to act upon the knowledge of faith, we begin to make wise, ethically sound decisions that

---

43.   From *True Spirituality* by Francis A. Schaeffer. © by Tyndale House Publishers, Inc. All rights reserved. Reprinted in 1991 by Crossway books as Vol. 3 of The Complete Works of Francis A. Shaeffer—A Christian Worldview. pp. 278-279.

honor God and produce the fruit of our union. The fruit of the heart that follows after God will be expressed in the decisions, priorities, and activities of daily life. Perhaps the most realistic life-example of applied wisdom is the description by the writer of Proverbs of a person who feared the Lord and whose life-pattern displayed this characteristic.

> **As we continue to act upon the knowledge of faith, we begin to make wise, ethically sound decisions that honor God and produce the fruit of our union. The fruit of the heart that follows after God will be expressed in the decisions, priorities, and activities of daily life.**

It is the description of the Proverbs 31 woman.

The character of this noble woman shines through all the activities of her busy life. The quality of her character cannot be measured by an itemized list of activities nor is the beauty of her character judged by cosmetic charm. She is wise in the depth of her being because she fears the Lord. She surpasses women who do "noble things" and her beauty does not fade with age. The closest to her see in her an example of God's grace and strength. Her family benefits from her confidence, discernment, and diligence. She has exchanged the flattery of superficial compliments for the praise of her character. This woman desires and demonstrates a discerning heart in everything she does.

Her life exemplifies the multifaceted nature of true wisdom; it touches every area of life. She can work with her hands as well as with her mind. She is active in the home and outside the home. She cares for her family materially and spiritually. Yet she does not live entirely for her family. She gives to the poor and needy as well. There is consistency and a coherence to her lifestyle. She is balanced but not bored, active but not hassled. She lives without excuses. Her spirituality is woven into the fabric of her life. She refuses to compartmentalize her activity into spiritual and secular categories. Her Mondays are as holy as her Sabbaths.

All we see in this woman of noble character presents a beautiful portrait of wisdom's harmony. She is fulfilled within herself but not by herself. She is one with her husband and supportive of her children. Her life in all its dimensions is its own reward! She is worthy of praise. But her real reward is in her work, in her relationships, in the experience of God's wisdom in her life. She does not do things to get them over with so she can get on with her life. Her fear of the Lord and humble service to the poor save her from self-righteousness.[44]

This is not just a picture of any woman, but a picture of the bride of Christ—one who has made herself ready. And it is granted to her to be arrayed in fine

---

44.   Webster, op. cit. pp. 102-103.

linen, clean and bright, for the fine linen is the righteous acts of the saints (see Rev. 19:7-8).

The Bridegroom spoke the words of wisdom in the Sermon on the Mount. He began with the beginning of wisdom, the fear (worshipping submission) of the Lord (see Mt. 5:3), and ended with how a wise man builds (see Mt. 7:24-27). Within the context of this Scripture, Jesus expounded on how a disciple's righteousness needs to exceed a mere outward observance (see Mt. 5:20). One's conceptual knowledge of God would be united with the experiential knowledge of God, which would produce a spiritual life that would be centered on the Word of God. The end picture of wisdom was revealed as the Church, the bride, a spiritual house, where wisdom hewed out her seven pillars (see Prov. 9:1) where the image of the visible Christ comes and challenges us to live in unity, forgiven that we might become holy, obedient (an example to others), and faithful.

> The fundamental dynamics of how to make moral choices are the same today as they were 2,000 or 3,000 years ago. ...Perhaps it would help to point out the four levels on which the Bible can relate to issues that you face. The first level is *prohibitions:* instructions that are clear and straight-forward, apply directly and une-quivocally to specific areas of life, and state mostly in the negative, in terms of what you must not do. "You shall not murder"(Ex. 20:13) is an example of a biblical prohibition.

A second level has to do with the Bible's *positive commands*. These are easy to understand and speak to broad, general areas of behavior. Applying them to a specific situation may take some thought and creativity. "Walk in love" (Eph. 5:2) is a positive command. So is "Husbands, love your wives, just as Christ also loved the church" (Eph. 5:25).

A third level of biblical instruction is *values and principles*. (Principles are basic truths taught by the Bible that apply to life.) The fourth level is the area of *conscience*. Matters of conscience occur when there are no clear prohibitions of Scripture that apply unequivocally to a situation. Instead, you have to forge a response out of whatever positive commands and principles you believe apply. In this area God leaves you with a great deal of latitude in what you decide to do. Applying these four levels of biblical instruction to life is what the Bible calls *wisdom,* which literally means "the skill of living.[45]

Skill takes time to develop; however, the Holy Spirit will enable us to discern truth as we apply the Word of God to our lives. This produces a freedom in us and allows us to align our words with our deeds, while we give God the allegiance of our hearts. Therefore, the ultimate ethical purpose is fulfilled—the

---

45. Doug Sherman and William Hendricks, *Keeping Your Ethical Edge Sharp* (Colorado Springs, Colorado: Navpress, 1990), pp. 146-147.

praise of God. God is praised as His will is done. Obedience is the means to achieve this goal. The grace of God empowers us to fulfill our moral imperative.

Conclusion

The word *ethics* comes from the Greek *ethos* meaning "foundation" or "root" and has to do with the philosophical basis for morality. It encompasses the reasons why certain behavioral patterns are perceived or accepted as more appropriate than others. Unlike morality which is concerned with what is actually taking place, ethics focuses on what ought to be done. Since the Christian perspective holds that people are required to do what they ought to do, what they ought to do being determined by God, the distinction between ethics and morality is significant for the Christian. A Christian's moral acts should be defined by godly ethics, which are Christ-centered.

The fact that God is righteous—or always "in the right"—is both a challenge and a comfort. The challenge comes to mankind through the realization that the rightness of human action must be determined not by the fluctuating moral standards of a volatile society, but by the unchanging revelation of an eternal God. The comfort of knowing that God is always "in the right" is found in the experience of the humble person who, though inconsistently turning to the Lord for wisdom when surrounded by an endless stream of contradictions, does turn and discovers that truth can be known and that right still exists.

This comfort, however, is frequently short-lived because the chasm that emerges between knowing what is right and doing what is right is oftentimes vast. The closer a man gets to the righteousness of God, the more uncomfortable he becomes about his own righteousness. In our search for truth, we see how unable we are to live it, and we either deny what is right because we can't live it in our own strength, or we turn to the enablement of God and try to live it—we run the race.

The gospel, however, recognizes this and in its revelation of the righteousness of God shows how the one who is not "in the right" before God can have his situation rectified. Through a transforming process, as illustrated in Figure 1, man is restored to the image of God through an obedience to the will of God that enables man to be brought into a relationship with God; out of this relationship come direction, destiny, and the enablement to fulfill that destiny. Ultimately, God is praised, which is the goal of all human conduct. God is praised as His will is done. Obedience is thus the means to achieve the goal, and a relationship with God is the means through which we achieve obedience.

Nevertheless, God's glory does not remain alone; for the glory of God means also the glorifying of the creature (see Rom. 8:17,30; 2 Cor. 3:18), a demonstration of His ongoing love for us. This glorifying is linked with the "spirit of sonship" that is given to all children of God, who by faith are joined to Christ (Rom. 8:15-17) through the cross. Human beings are thus brought into union with God both *in being and in act*—a union that embraces union with fellow believers (see Eph. 4:4-16). In the obedient doing of the will of God, one achieves the authentic humanity or being in the divine image, which God planned for men and women in His creative work. Since the divine mandate at creation included dominion over other creatures (see Gen. 1:26), the proper ordering and curatorship of the physical environment forms a part of theological ethics in accordance with its goal in God (see Rom. 8:18-22).

In regard to our goal, as well as ground, norm, and power, Holy Scripture plays a key role, for it is only through the inspired record of God that God, as the goal of human action, may be known and accepted, with all that this implies for the direction of life, the course and validity of right action, and the destiny of those who commit themselves to God as their all in all.

Finally truth, as revealed by God, requires wisdom in its application. The illustration in Figure 2 shows the tension that is needed to hold on to truth. At the extremes we find legalism and antinomianism; either side is error. As we discern truth, we must search out its foundation, the seed from which it was brought forth, as well as look at the results or fruit that a truth has produced. Man's desire to walk in truth is reflective of God's creative work. God, who is truth, created man in His image to reflect truth in his daily walk. Man was to know truth through his experiential relationship with God (e.g., God and Adam walking together in the cool of the day—what experience were they sharing?) and not by thoughts and reasonings exclusive of God. With this in mind, we hide the Word of God in our heart for it is a light unto our path. The Word of God directs our experiential walk with God. The more the truth of the Word is revealed the more we can experience God who is truth; the more we experience the truth, the closer we come to our quest—not only to know the truth but to walk in truth. Let us continue to walk in the light on the narrow road prepared for us.

ETHICAL PURPOSE

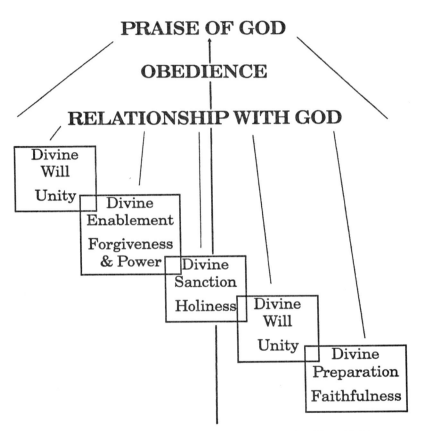

PRAISE OF GOD

OBEDIENCE

RELATIONSHIP WITH GOD

Divine
Will

Unity

Divine
Enablement

Forgiveness
& Power

Divine
Sanction

Holiness

Divine
Will

Unity

Divine
Preparation

Faithfulness

TRANSFORMING PROCESS
MADE IN THE IMAGE OF GOD

TO BE → TO KNOW → TO DO

Figure 1

Error	Truth	Error
Legalism (Misues God's Law)	God created man to be conformed to the image of Jesus Christ (Romans 8:29)	**Antinomianism** (Lawlessness)
1. Abstracts the law of God from its original context.	The image of Jesus Christ is found in the morality of God. He wants that morality to be ours	1. **Libertinism:** Liberated from law (license to sin).
2. Add legislation to God's law and treat the addition as if it were divine law (Mark 7:1-13).	As God's people we can know truth (John 8:32).	2. **Gnostic spiritualism:** "Gnostic"– knowledge claim – special or hidden knowledge – exempt – biblical rules "higher class"
When this happens, people presumptuously and arrogantly usurp the authority of God.	Truth needs to be held in tension—this requires wisdom.	3. **Situation ethics:** Depends on situation.
	Truth gives us direction so that we do the will of God which is good and acceptable and perfect (Romans 12:2).	

Figure 2

Discussions Questions

1. How does the task of Christian ethics differ from all other ethics?

2. Why is unity an important consideration in establishing a foundation for Christian ethics?

3. Consider forgiveness as a means of enablement.

   a. What is meant by receiving God's grace?

   b. How does it enable you to fulfill God's will?

4. Why is the concept of holiness an important consideration in living and defining a Christian ethic?

5. In considering our divine mission to be a witness.

   a. How do you reconcile the difference between an individual and corporate responsibility?

   b. How is the Body of Christ made visible?

6. Through Scripture there is a special relationship between God and His people. The apostle Paul describes this relationship as a bridegroom with his bride. Using the analogy of marriage, how are we as a people of God being prepared for Him?

7. Wisdom is defined as skillful living, how might we increase our ability to live skillfully?

References

Chapter 1

1. Protagoras of Abera

Born: c. 490 B.C., possibly in Abdera, Greece
Died: c. 420 B.C., possibly by drowning at sea
Major Works: *On Truth, On the Gods* (only fragments remain)

Major Ideas

Educated persons are skilled in the art of rhetoric, which enables them to articulate thought with clarity and superior argumentation.

What enables one to lead others can be taught.

No one is absolutely self-sufficient, for human survival depends on mutual cooperation in society—hence the importance of values, communication, and laws.

Because all have a basic need for self-preservation, all have the obligation to participate in the governance of the community.

Man is the measure of all things: Perception and truth are relative to the experience and judgment of the individual.

One cannot with certainty either affirm or reject the existence of the gods.

> Ian P. McGreal, ed., *Great Thinkers of the Western World* (New York, New York: Harper Collins Publishers, 1992), p. 12.

2. Aristotle

Born: 384 B.C., Stageira, in Thrace
Died: 322 B.C., Chalcis, in Euboea

Major Ideas

Ideas do not have an independent, extra-mental subsistence, but exist in things.

The material substratum, which is the potential for the existence of finite things, must be distinguished from abolute nonbeing or privation.

The substances of things are a union of form and matter.

Body and soul are conjoined as matter and form.

The existence of all finite and transitory things can be understood as a movement from potential to actual existence.

The world exists eternally, and movement of all things is an unceasing movement.

The source of this movement is the unmoved or eternally actual First Mover, the actuality of which draws finite things from potential into actual existence.

The emirical order is a suitable realm for inquiry based on sense perception; whereas in the logical order, demonstration proceeds inductively from the observed particular to general conclusions.

The "good" is "that at which all things aim."

All human inquiry and behavior is, therefore, guided by its end or goal, which is a particular good.

Ian P. McGreal, ed., *Great Thinkers of the Western World* (New York, New York: Harper Collins Publishers, 1992), p. 30.

Chapter 2

1. James Orr

The son of an engineer named Robert Orr, James was born in Glasgow on April 11, 1844. After graduating from the university in his home city, he studied at the Divinity Hall of the University of Edinburgh from which he received his B.D. Later the University of Glasgow granted him a D.D. simply on examination, which was an extraordinary feat of scholarship. He served the East Bank Presbyterian Church in Hawick for 17 years, diligently studying while faithfully pastoring. In 1891 he was invited to give the first series of Kerr Lectures which were later published under the title, *The Christian View of God and the World*. In 1891 he was appointed to the chair of Church History at his *alma mater* in Edinburgh. In 1900 he took the chair of Apologetics and Systematic Theology in Glasgow where he remained until his death on September 6, 1913.

James Orr, *The Christian View of God and the World* (Grand Rapids, Michigan: Kregel Publications, reprinted 1989).

Chapter 3

1. Peter Abelard

Born: 1079, Le Pallet, near Nantes, France
Died: 1142, Saint Marcel Monastery, near Chalon, France

Major Ideas

Universals, while not real in and of themselves, have a linguistic and intellectual reality that derives from their participation in particulars.

Authority, while essential, is by itself insufficient to an understanding of dogma; reason must understand dogma by analogies from the material world.

The classics of pre-Christian philosophy are informed by God and contain mystical prefigurations of Christian thinking.

Seemingly opposed views within the authoritative deposit of the faith can often be reconciled by observing the development of a thought throughout the works of the authors in question, by the establishment of best texts, and by the application of hermeneutical dialectic.

Intentions, not deeds, count before God; human works are morally indifferent and do nothing to secure either merit or blame.

The power to bind or loose sins is held only by those discreet and holy bishops who are worthy successors of the apostles.

> Ian P. McGreal, ed., *Great Thinkers of the Western World* (New York, New York: Harper Collins Publishers, 1992), p. 87.

2. William of Ockham

Born: c. 1285, probably in the village of Ockham in the county of Surrey, near London
Died: c. 1347, Munich (probably of the Black Death)

Major Ideas

Nominalism rejects the view that there are universals (essences) in things; it emphasizes the experienced world of contingent beings.

The name used for a thing does not capture the essence of the thing but is simply a conventional sign used to refer to the thing.

Logic seeks to organize and clarify human thought.

Intuitive cognition is a certain grasp by sense and judgment of any particular being, while abstractive cognition based on intuitive cognition organizes many similar things under universal terms (names).

Ockham's razor is the principle of economy in theorizing; it calls for the least number of assumptions in the construction of an explanation.

God is known by faith in His revelation, not by examining His creation.

Creation and salvation are the manifestations of the divine will that call each person to a covenant partnership.

The claim of the papacy to be supreme over the secular realm is to be rejected.

The gospel law is the law of freedom.

> Ian P. McGreal, ed., *Great Thinkers of the Western World* (New York, New York: Harper Collins Publishers, 1992), p. 123.

3. Jerry Bentham

Born: 1748, London, England
Died: 1832, London, England

Major Ideas

Human beings are motivated solely by the desire to gain pleasure and avoid pain.

The morality of our actions is determined by their utility.

Happiness is identical with pleasure, unhappiness with pain.

Pleasure alone is intrinsically good (good in itself) and pain alone is intrisically bad.

We have a duty to promote the pleasure of every individual equally.

Pleasures differ from one another only in quantity, never in quality.

Human behavior is controlled by the imposition of sanctions.

Justice requires equality but is subordinate to utility.

> Ian P. McGreal, ed., *Great Thinkers of the Western World* (New York, New York: Harper Collins Publishers, 1992), p. 306.

4. John Stuart Mill

Born: 1806, London, England
Died: 1873, Avignon, France

Major Ideas

All knowledge is derived orginally from sense perception.

Matter, or the eternal world, can be defined as the permanent possibility of sensation.

Mind is reducible to sucessive conscious states.

True inference is always accomplished through induction rather than deduction.

Pleasure alone is intrinsically good and pain alone is intrisically bad.

Pleasure differs from each other qualitatively as well as quantitatively, a "higher" pleasure being intrinsically better than a "lower" pleasure.

The only justification society has in interfering with the liberty of action of any individual is self-protection.

Given the existence of evil, God cannot be both omnipotent and morally good; if He exists, He must be limited in power.

Ian P. McGreal, ed., *Great Thinkers of the Western World* (New York, New York: Harper Collins Publishers, 1992), p. 360.

5. Soren Kierkegaard

Born: 1813, Copenhagen, Denmark
Died: 1855, Copenhagen, Denmark

Major Ideas

As human beings, we are often in situations in which we must choose between incompatible alternatives.

God may place us religiously in paradoxical situations of anguished choice as a test of faith.

There are objective problems, but they cannot be answered objectively for the person, who must decide about his or her subjective relation.

We live aesthetically without commitment, but ethical situations demand decisions from us that are decisive.

The individual is more important than the universal.

Uncertainty permeates human life and is only overcome by human decisiveness.

Paradox stands at the center of all human existence.

The essential self lives inwardly in ways that cannot be given full outward expression.

Ian P. McGreal, ed., *Great Thinkers of the Western World* (New York, New York: Harper Collins Publishers, 1992), p. 369.

6. Friedrich Nietzsche

Born: 1844, Rocken, Germany
Died: 1900, Weimar, Germany

Major Ideas

Self-deception is a particularly destructive characteristic of Western culture.

Life is the will to power; our natural desire is to dominate and to reshape the world to fit our own preferences and to assert our personal strength to the fullest degree possible.

Struggle, through which individuals achieve a degree of power commensurate with their abilities, is the basic fact of human existence.

Ideals of human equality perpetuate mediocrity—a truth that has been distorted and concealed by modern value systems.

Christian morality, which identifies goodness with meekness and servility, is the prime culprit in creating a cultural climate that thwarts the drive for excellence and self-realization.

God is dead; a new era of human creativity and achievement is at hand.

> Ian P. McCreal, ed., *Great Thinkers of the Western World* (New York, New York: Harper Collins Publishers, 1992), p. 408.

7. Jean-Paul Sartre

Born: 1905, Paris, France
Died: 1980, Paris, France

Major Ideas

For human beings, "existence precedes essence"; we are defined by our choices and actions and not by a fixed "human nature."

The direction a person's life will take is always in ques
tion and a matter of contingency.

We exist in situations—typically these are interpersonal and social—and they affect us; but how we exist
within them is decisively a matter of our choosing.

The radical freedom that permeates our lives make us
responsible for ourselves and for one another; it also
means that a complete and final understanding of ourselves eludes us.

Our freedom confers immense responsibility, and thus
people often live in "bad faith," evading responsibility
for their lives by denying the reality of their own
freedom.

> Ian P. McGreal, ed., *Great Thinkers of the Western
> World* (New York, New York: Harper Collins Pub-
> lishers, 1992), p. 541.

8. Charles Darwin

Born: 1809, Shrewesbury, England
Died: 1882, Downe, Kent, England

Major Ideas

Species are related to each other by descent, with the
changes from their common ancestors being caused by
the survival and reproduction of advantageous genetic
variants.

Overpopulation and the resulting shortage of food create the pressure that causes organisms that have advantageous genetic variants to produce a greater
number of surviving offspring than those that do not
have these variants.

Man and apes are descended from a common primate
ancestor.

Secondary sexual characteristics have evolved as part of a complex set of reproductive behaviors.

Ian P. McGreal, ed., *Great Thinkers of the Western World* (New York, New York: Harper Collins Publishers, 1992), p. 364.

Bibliography

Angeles, Peter A. *Dictionary of Philosophy.* New York, New York: Harper Perennial, 1991.

Bahnsen, Greg L. *Theonomy in Christian Ethics.* Phillipsburg, New Jersey: Presbyterian and Reformed Publishing Company, 1984.

Barlow, N. *Autobiography of Charles Darwin.* London, England: Collins, 1958.

Bonhoeffer, Dietrich, in Eberhard Bethge (ed.) *Ethics.* New York, New York: Macmillan Publishing Company, 1986.

Briscoe, Stuart D. *The Communicator's Commentary: Romans.* Waco, Texas: Word Books, Publisher, 1982.

Bromiley, G.W. "Philosophical Ethics: Nature and Function," *The International Standard Bible Encyclopedia.* Grand Rapids, Michigan: William B. Eerdmans Publishing Company, reprinted 1988.

Bruce, F.F. *Tyndale New Testament Commentaries: Romans.* Grand Rapids, Michigan: William B. Eerdmans Publishing Company, reprinted 1988.

Chafer, Lewis Sperry. *Major Bible Themes*. Grand Rapids, Michigan: Zondervan Publishing House, 1974.

Conner, Kevin J. *The Church in the New Testament*. Portland, Oregon: Bible Temple Publishing, 1975.

Cunningham, James D. and Anthony C. Fortosis. *Education in the Christian Schools: A Perspective and Training Model*. Whittier, California: The Association of Christian Schools International, 1987.

DeKoster, Lester "Liberation Theology Adopts Marxism" *Family Protection Scoreboard Magazine*, 1989. Chart prepared by Raneld A. Hunsicker. Published by National Citizens Action Network, Costa Mesa, California.

Ediger, Walter O. *The Quest for Excellence in Christian School Education*. Siloam Springs, Arizona: RPA Associates, 1993.

Foulkes, Francis. *Tyndale New Testament Commentaries: Ephesians*. Grand Rapids, Michigan: William B. Eerdmans Publishing Company, 1989.

Geisler, Norman L. *Christian Ethics: Options and Issues*. Grand Rapids, Michigan: Baker Book House, 1990.

Harless, G. Chr. Adolph von *System of Christian Ethics*. Edinburgh: T. & T. Clark, 1887.

Harrison, R.K. (ed.) *Encyclopedia of Biblical and Christian Ethics*. Nashville, Tennessee: Thomas Nelson Publishers, 1987.

Harris, Ralph W. (ed.) *The New Testament Study Bible: Romans—Corinthians*. The Complete Bible Library, 1989. Springfield, Missouri.

Henry, Carl F.H. *Christian Personal Ethics*. Grand Rapids, Michigan: William B. Eerdmans Publishing Company, 1957.

Henry, Carl F.H. *The Christian Mindset in a Secular Society*. Portland, Oregon: Multnomah Press, 1984.

Huxley, Julian., in Rogers E. Greeley (ed.) *The Best of Humanism*. Buffalo, New York: Prometheus Books, 1988.

Iverson, Dick. Spring Conference Notes, *Holiness: The Unique Escape from Oblivion*. New York, New York: Ministers Fellowship International, 1992.

Iverson, Dick. *Present Day Truths*. Portland, Oregon: Bible Temple Publishing, 1975.

Jastrow, Robert. *God and the Astronomers*. New York: W.W. Norton, 1978.

Kaiser, Walter C. *Toward Old Testament Ethics*. Grand Rapids, Michigan: Zondervan Publishing House, 1983.

Keyser, Leander S. *A Manual of Christian Ethics*. Iowa: The Lutheran Literary Board, 1926.

Kruse, Colin. *Tyndale New Testament Commentaries: II Corinthians*. Grand Rapids, Michigan: William B. Eerdmans Publishing Company, 1989.

Lucado, Max. *The Applause of Heaven*. Dallas, Texas: Word Publishing, 1990.

MacLennan, W.D.G. *Christian Obedience*. London, England: Thomas Nelson and Sons Ltd., 1948.

McClendon, James Wm., Jr. *Ethics: Systematic Theology*. Nashville, Tennessee: Abingdon Press, 1986.

McDowell, William H. and R.C. Sproul, Jr. *Battle for Our Minds: Worldviews in Collision, Study Guide*. Orlando, Florida: Ligonier Ministries, 1992.

McGreal, Ian P., ed. *Great Thinkers of the Western World* New York, New York: Harper Collins Publishers, 1992.

Mott, Stephen. *Biblical Ethics and Social Change*. New York: Oxford University Press, 1982.

Nicole, Roger R. "Authority," in Carl F.H. Henry (ed.) *Baker's Dictionary of Christian Ethics*. Grand Rapids, Michigan: Baker Book House, 1973.

Noebel, David A. *Understanding the Times*. Manitou Springs, Colorado: Summit Press, 1992.

Orr, James. *The Christian View of God and the World*. Grand Rapids, Michigan: Kregel Publications, reprinted 1989.

Sahakian, William S. *History Of Philosophy*. New York, New York: Harper Collins Publishers, 1968.

Schaeffer, Francis A. "A Christian View of Spirituality," *The Complete Works of Francis A. Schaeffer—A Christian Worldview*. Wheaton, Illinois: Crossway Books, reprinted 1991.

Sciacca, Fran. *Generation at Risk*. Minneapolis, Minnesota: World Wide Publications, 1990.

Sherman, Doug and Willian Hendricks. *Keeping Your Ethical Edge Sharp*. Colorado Springs, Colorado: Navpress, 1990.

Sire, James W. *The Universe Next Door*. Downers Grade, Illinois: InterVarsity Press, 1988.

Smith, Wolfgang. *Teihardism and the New Religion*. Rockford, Illinois: Tan Books, 1988.

Sproul, R.C. *Lifeviews*. Old Tappan, New Jersey: Fleming H. Revell Company, 1986.

Trueblood, D. Elton. *Philosophy of Religion*. Grand Rapids, Michigan: Baker Book House, 1975.

Walker, George. *The Idealism of Christian Ethics*. Edinburgh: T. & T. Clark Co., 1929.

Webster, Douglas D. *Choices of the Heart: Christian Ethics for Today*. Grand Rapids, Michigan: Zondervan Publishing House, 1990.

Webster's II New Riverside University Dictionary. Boston, Massachusetts: The Riverside Publishing Company, 1984.